An exploration of the relationship of ego development theory to counselor development

Leslie DiAnne Borders

TABLE OF CONTENTS

LIST OF TABLES

Abstract of Dissertation Presented to the Graduate
School of the University of Florida in Partial
Fulfillment of the Requirements for the Degree
of Doctor of Philosophy

AN EXPLORATION OF THE RELATIONSHIP OF EGO DEVELOPMENT
THEORY TO COUNSELOR DEVELOPMENT

By

Leslie DiAnne Borders

August 1984

Chairperson: Dr. Margaret L. Fong
Cochairperson: Dr. P. Joseph Wittmer
Major Department Counselor Education

This study explored the efficacy of the theory of ego

development as a theoretical basis for developmental models

of supervision. A review of the literature of supervision

education indicated a need for a theoretical explanation of

individual differences in counselor development and pointed

to the relevance of ego development to counselor development.

The level of ego development for 63 graduate counseling

students was assessed by the Sentence Completion Test. Mul-

tiple dependent measures of counseling variables were in-

cluded: the structure (cognitive complexity, integration,

meaningfulness) and the content of perceptions of clients

were measured by the Repertory Grid Technique; in-session

counseling behavior with clients, by the Vanderbilt Psycho-

therapy Process Scales, and individual supervisors' ratings

of overall effectiveness, by the Counselor Evaluation Rating

Scale. A series of five separate multiple regression analyses were computed to test the relationship of students' levels of ego development with the structural cognitive measures of their perceptions and in-session behavior and overall effectiveness ratings. None of the computed partial correlations were significant at the .05 set-wise criterion level

A 3 (ego level) X 4 (content category) Chi-square test of differences for the content of perceptions of clients was significant, indicating counseling students at higher ego levels used fewer physical descriptions and more interactional style descriptions. Post-hoc analysis suggested the interaction of cognitive complexity and integration scores tended to be related to ego levels. A highly complex relationship may exist between students' ego levels and their cognitions about clients.

There were near significant positive relationships of counseling students' in-session behavior and supervisors' overall effectiveness ratings with ego levels. Level of experience appeared to have a mediating effect on scores on several variables.

The strength of the relationships between levels of ego development and scores on the counseling variables provides tentative support for the theoretical hypotheses of the relationships between ego development and counselor development and suggests further research in this area. The results also provide some support for developmental models of supervision. Limitations of the study, implications for counselor development, and recommendations for future research are discussed

CHAPTER I
INTRODUCTION

Supervision has frequently been conceptualized as an educational process by which supervisors continue to "teach" counseling to their supervisees beyond classroom training in basic skills (Leddick & Bernard, 1980). Theorists and researchers have offered varied explanations for how students learn to become counselors, how supervisors function as educators in the learning process, and the desired learning goals of supervision (for example, see Bartlett, Goodyear, & Bradley, 1983, Hart, 1982; Hess, 1980a). Whatever the role (i.e., teacher, counselor, consultant) ascribed to the supervisor by theorists, the goal of supervision has been an educational one: promoting student learning in one or more areas such as counseling skills, self-awareness, or counselor-client interactions.

These supervision theories have been criticized for being primarily adjuncts to counseling theories, however, rather than distinct theories of supervision education (Bartlett, 1983); for being "metaphors of experience" rather than scientifically established theories (Holloway & Hosford, 1983, p. 75). This view has led some reviewers of supervision literature to conclude there is a lack of a theoretical base for supervision education (Holloway &

1

Hosford, 1983, Leddick & Bernard, 1980; Mahon & Altmann, 1977). Holloway and Hosford (1983), however, have noted that recent developmental models of supervision do not equate the counseling and supervision process and relationships, but differentiate "between the process of counseling and the process of becoming a counselor" (p. 73). They believe these developmental models offer a framework for a systematic approach to research which can provide the empirical evidence for a sound theory of supervision education.

Developmental Models of Supervision Education

The developmental models describe supervision as a process of successive stages and highlight the educational nature of supervision. These models present counselor growth as a progression of sequential, hierarchial stages, each of which requires different supervision instruction strategies. Developmental theorists vary in their base for describing the stages of counselor growth: Littrell, Lee-Borden, and Lorenz (1979) focus on the changing roles or functions of the supervisor; Loganbill, Hardy, and Delworth (1982) describe the dynamics of the supervisee confronting developmental tasks or issues; Blocher (1983) and Stoltenberg (1981) discuss environmental and personal variables impacting the learning process. Recent studies based on the concepts of the developmental models of supervision evidence some progress in a systematic approach to supervision research, although few studies have attempted to actually validate a model

A recent study based on Stoltenberg's model (Miars, Tracey, Ray, Cornfeld, O'Farrell, & Gelso, 1983) found supervisors perceived themselves varying their behaviors with supervisees at different experience levels. They perceived themselves offering inexperienced supervisees (first or second semester practicum) more structure, direction, support, and teaching, while emphasizing personal development, client resistance, and transference/counter-transference issues with more experienced supervisees (advanced practicum or intern level). The authors concluded the supervisors were clearly "making some kind of developmental distinctions when describing the nature of their supervision across various trainee levels" (p. 410). Even though the variations closely paralleled the optimal supervision educational environments proposed by Stoltenberg (1981), the authors could not specify from their data what distinctions the supervisors were using to make decisions about their supervisory behavior. The supervisors also seemed to make more "gross developmental distinctions" (p. 410) (two levels) than those postulated by Stoltenberg (four levels).

Other research related to developmental models has focused on counselors' perceptions of their supervisors. Differences were found among counselors at various experience levels in several of these studies. Worthington and

Roehlke (1979), for example, found beginning counselors (the only experience level included) preferred direct teaching and structured supervision within a supportive relationship. Cross and Brown (1983) reported counselors at different experience levels perceived their supervisors as behaving differently. Beginning counselors perceived their supervisors as emphasizing tasks and methods while experienced counselors felt their supervisors' behaviors created a more supportive and more intense relationship. During post-hoc interviews following a longitudinal study by Hill, Charles and Reed (1981), counselors reported changes in their relationships with their supervisors over time, moving from dependency and anxiety about the supervisors' judgments and evaluations to a more peer-like, consultative relationship.

These studies provide some support for developmental models of supervision; both supervisees and supervisors report and/or evidence changes in the supervision process over time But the stages of the developmental models of supervision of Stoltenberg (1981) and Loganbill et al. (1982) are not based on experience levels alone. Instead they emphasize individual variations in counselor progress through the developmental stages and imply personal attributes will affect a counselor's rate of progress.

The developmental models which highlight the dynamics of the supervisee and the learning process offer some explanations for the individual variations in development. Loganbill et al. (1982) assume counselors will function at

different competency levels (stages) with each of the eight
developmental issues they describe. Blocher (1983) believes
one strength of his model is its capacity to adjust to
students' individual differences in learning styles and
current developmental stage. Stoltenberg (1981) also recognizes variation in counselors' motivations, needs, and
potential resistances within each stage of development. His
model is based on the premise "that there are qualitative
differences in addition to, and not accounted for by, mere
quantitative differences in skill level and the knowledge
of theories" (p. 59). He states that development will vary
"significantly from trainee to trainee" (p. 60), depending
"on the skills and attributes of the trainee" (p. 63).

The confounding effects of individual differences has
been illustrated by Reising and Daniels' (1983) attempt to
validate Hogan's (1964) developmental model, the theoretical basis for Stoltenberg's (1981) developmental model.
Supervisees at four experience levels rated statements they
might make about themselves and statements they might make
about their supervision needs. The statements were designed
to reflect issues in the first three levels of Hogan's
model. While the supervisees' response patterns supported
Hogan's model of counselor development in general, the
authors concluded that a simple stage model could not adequately describe the complexity of the issues Hogan included.
The authors added, "supervisors may need to go beyond the
simple developmental model and examine how the complex

model's individual issues are organized within each trainee"
(p. 242).

Friedlander and Snyder (1983) included self-efficacy
expectations of counselors at various experience levels in
a study of outcome expectancies of supervision and expectations of supervisor's attributes and role. High levels
of confidence and high levels of expectations that supervision would affect clients predicted high expectations for
expert and evaluative supervisors; level of experience, however, was not predictive of expectations. Like Reising
and Daniels (1983), the authors concluded "individual differences override level of experience" (p. 348). It seems
that experience level alone is not sufficient to explain the
complexities of counselor growth and development.

The attention to individual differences to help explain
counselor development during supervision would be a significant contribution to theories of supervision. Reviewers of
supervision research have cited the need to investigate the
impact of the counselor's personal attributes on the learning process in supervision (Bartlett, 1983; Holloway &
Hosford, 1983; Lambert, 1980; Mahon & Altmann, 1977). The
developmental models, however, have not detailed the personal
attributes which may account for individual variation in
learning (i.e., Blocher, 1983; Stoltenberg, 1981). Stoltenberg (1981), for example, believes a supervisor should
consider an individual counselor's unique cognitive, motivational, value, and sensory orientations when creating an

appropriate learning environment, but his model does not
specify how these orientations may affect individual variations in counselor development. Stoltenberg has urged "a
further delineation of the characteristics of counselors at
different levels" (p. 64) which can better indicate appropriate choices of supervision learning environments and can
serve as a basis for future studies evaluating the effectiveness of different supervision techniques. He concluded,
"Once this task has been accomplished for all levels of
counselor trainees, the factors appearing to be most instrumental in effecting change during the supervision process
can be operationalized and subjected to empirical scrutiny"
(p. 64).

While the Loganbill et al. (1982) "conceptual model" is
systematic, integrative, and descriptive of supervisee
dynamics, Miller (1982) finds it limited by its failure to
delineate the internal psychological processes evolving in
counselors during development. He believes there are three
such underlying processes or personality traits: conceptual
and ego development, emotional flexibility and congruence,
and awareness. Concurrent development of the three in a
supervisee is essential, developing into a mature professional over at least a twenty-year span. Miller believes
a supervisor's use of "catalytic interventions will facilitate conceptual, emotional, and awareness shifts that will
be marked by movement through the various developmental

stages" (p. 48) which have not been adequately described by theorists.

Both Miller (1982) and Blocher (1983) name stage theorists whose work serves as the basis for their developmental approaches to supervision. Blocher (1983), however, does not integrate these theories into a sequential model of supervision, and Miller (1982) presents only a very concise overview of an integration of stage theory and counselor development. In addition, no studies to date have attempted to link counselor development with an established theory of personality development.

In sum, the individual personal attributes of a supervisee which could be critical for supervisors to consider in the learning process have not been specified in a detailed, comprehensive developmental model by either theorists or researchers. In addition, none of the developmental models have incorporated in detail a theoretical basis (i.e., personality theory) which could explain what internal psychological changes occur and how they occur in counselors as they integrate theoretical knowledge from the classroom with practical experience in practicum and internship experiences.

Ego Development

Loevinger's (Loevinger, 1966, 1976) concept of ego development and stages offers a comprehensive theoretical framework of personality development which could serve as a basis for counselor development. Loevinger defines ego development as the "master trait" which reflects a person's frame of reference for perceiving, interpreting, and reacting to others and one's life experiences.

Loevinger has integrated theories of self, cognitive, character, moral and interpersonal development (Hauser, 1976; Loevinger, 1976; Swenson, 1980a) into a stage theory which is marked by increasing differentiation and integration of views of the world, others, and self, and a shift from an external to an internal focus. For instance, a person's interpersonal style moves from dependency to manipulation to belongingness to mutuality. Loevinger describes this development in a series of ten major stages and transition levels labeled by somewhat descriptive terms, as summarized in Table 1.

One's perceptions of the world, others, and self are reflected in a cognitive, moral, and interpersonal style characteristic of a level of ego development. Loevinger's (Loevinger & Wessler, 1970) detailed descriptions of the cognitive and interpersonal styles of persons at different levels of ego development imply counselors at different ego levels would have varying capacities to, among other things, express empathy, respect a client's differentness, deal with identity issues, and understand the interactive dynamics of the counselor-client relationship.

A substantial body of literature has offered evidence of construct validity for the theory of ego development,

TABLE 1

STAGES OF EGO DEVELOPMENT

Code	Name and Characteristics of Stage
I-0	Presocial. The stage characteristic of newborn infants and severely regressed psychotics, in which a person is unable to distinguish self from others. Behavior is motivated by immediate impulses.
I-1	Symbiotic. A prespeech stage in which a person does not clearly differentiate self from others. Interpersonal relations are symbiotic and behavior is still motivated by immediate impulses.
I-2	Impulsive. A stage in which a person begins to establish a separate identity; is dependent, demanding, egocentric and conceptually simplistic; and sees others as primarily sources of supply. Behavior is governed by rules and punishment; problems are external, and recognized emotions are in a limited range.
Delta	Self-protective. A stage in which the main motivation is not getting caught and control is a major theme. A person is opportunistic, manipulative, and hedonistic, but also less impulsive and dependent. Problems are blamed on others or circumstances.
Delta/3	(Unnamed). A transitional stage in which the most predominant theme is concrete, traditional sex roles. A person's obedience and conformity to social norms is based in simple and absolute rules. Emotions are quasi-physiological; cleanliness and physical appearance are stressed.
I-3	Conformist. A stage in which a person's major motivation is following the rules, being concerned with reputation, social acceptance, appearance, and disapproval. Others are described in stereotypic terms and moralistic cliches, and one's inner life is viewed in generalized and banal terms. Interpersonal interaction is described in terms of behaviors.

TABLE 1. Continued.

Code	Name and Characteristics of Stage
I-3/4	Self-aware. A transitional stage in which a person allows exceptions to rules and perceives multiple possibilities in situations, although still in terms of stereotypic categories. The increase in self-consciousness and self-awareness allows some differentiation of self from the group. Interpersonal interactions are described in terms of feelings or traits. This is probably the modal level of young adults (ages 18-25) (Loevinger & Knoll, 1983).
I-4	Conscientious. A stage in which a person is preoccupied with achievement and responsibility, and self-criticism and self-evaluation by internalized moral principles. A person has a richly differentiated inner life, a sense of a longer time perspective, and a greater ability to differentiate between others. Psychological causality is understood. Interpersonal relations are based on the deeper feelings and needs of others. This may be the modal stage for most graduate students (Swenson, 1980b).
I-4/5	Individualistic. A transitional stage in which a person is increasingly aware of conflicts between others' needs and one's own needs, and of their own internal conflicts. Major themes are a heightened sense of individuality and a concern for emotional independence. Interpersonal relationships are valued and are seen as continuing or changing over time. There is a distinction between process and outcome.
I-5	Autonomous. A stage of cognitive complexity in which a person is able to transcend polarities and appreciate paradoxes. Individual differences are cherished; conflict is accepted as part of the human condition. A person recognizes the need of others for autonomy and allows others to be herself or himself. A person has a high tolerance for ambiguity; is preoccupied with self-fulfillment and wants to be realistic, objective, and unprejudiced.

TABLE 1. Continued.

Code	Name and Characteristics of Stage
I-6	Integrated. A stage in which a person promotes the growth and development of others, having accepted and learned to cope with complexities and paradoxes. The major focus is achieving an integrated identity. There is existential humor, value for justice, and idealism, and reconciliation to one's destiny. Few people have achieved this stage, which resembles Maslow's self-actualized person.

Note. Sources: Loevinger, 1979; Loevinger & Wessler, 1970; Swenson, 1977, 1980b.

including sequentiality and descriptions of behaviors and attitudes characterizing each stage (Hauser, 1976, Loevinger, 1979; Loevinger & Wessler, 1970).

Several authors have commented on ego development theory's relevance to counseling and counselor development (Blocher, 1983; Miller, 1982; Swenson, 1977, 1980a). Swenson (1977), for example, views ego development as "the central personality variable in interpersonal relations" (p. 41). Both Miller (1982) and Blocher (1983) specify Loevinger as one of the stage theorists whose work serves as the bases for their developmental approaches to supervision. Miller's (1982) developmental sequence closely parallels Loevinger's stages, and his final stage, also named "integration," is characterized by conceptual and ego complexity, emotional flexibility and congruence, and full awareness. Blocher's (1983) definition of a counselor at a high level of cognitive functioning, though couched in information-processing terms, also closely resembles Loevinger's description of the Integrated (I-6) person. His more cognitively complex counselor is able to take multiple perspectives and offer empathic understanding to a wider variety of clients because of their greater ability to differentiate and integrate a wide range of information. Blocher, however, does not outline a stage sequence of counselor development in his approach. Stoltenberg's (1981) descriptions of counselor characteristics at his four levels of development also

reflect characteristics of levels of ego development, although Stoltenberg does not refer to Loevinger's theory

Rationale for the Study

Ego development theory could provide a framework for
understanding, charting, and facilitating counselor development within the supervision process. It describes cognitive and interpersonal orientations which could have important implications for counselor education and supervision.
It describes issues counselors at different ego levels may
be confronting within themselves, issues which may color
their perceptions of and attitudes toward clients. It
describes both basal and optimal developmental levels for
counselors' ability to understand clients and their issues,
and for their ability to "perform" certain counseling skills.

By viewing supervision as an educational process and
raising a supervisee's level of ego development as one of
its educational goals, we have a potential basis for a
comprehensive theory of supervision education. Ego development may provide a theoretical basis for describing sequential stages of counselor growth in both the cognitive and
interpersonal domains. Theoretical application of ego
development to supervision to date has been fragmentary and
incomplete (i.e., Blocher, 1983; Miller, 1982), or implied
rather than explicitly stated (i.e , Stoltenberg, 1981).
Lacking is a comprehensive application of each level of ego
development to counselor cognitive and interpersonal orientations.

What seems to be needed is a descriptive list of perceptions and behaviors of counseling students at each level of ego development. Such a detailed description could provide a representation of progressive stages of counselor development and a way to tap into the internal changes in perceptions and attitudes counselors experience during their supervision experiences. It could provide a description of desired outcomes--the counselor perceptions, attitudes, and behaviors supervisors are aiming towards--and a way to assess the effectiveness of supervision education. It could also provide a measure to assess a counselor's progress and development.

Purpose of the Study

The purpose of the proposed study is to explore the usefulness of applying the theory of ego development to counselor development and supervision education. The study will examine the theory's ability to differentiate between counseling students at different ego levels in terms of perception of their clients, behaviors with their clients, and counseling effectiveness with their clients.

Statement of the Problem

The proposed study will address the need to describe the effects of counseling students' personal attributes on their learning process, and the need for a theoretical basis to explain the psychological, perceptual and behavioral

changes in counseling students during the learning process.
More specifically, the study will attempt to answer the
following research questions:

1. Is there a relationship between students' levels of
ego development and the level of cognitive complexity of
their perceptions of their clients?

2   Is there a relationship between students' levels of
ego development and the level of cognitive integration of
their perceptions of their clients?

3. Is there a relationship between students' levels of
ego development and the level of meaningfulness of their
perceptions of their clients?

4. Is there a relationship between students' levels of
ego development and their behavior with their clients?

5. Is there a relationship between students' levels of
ego development and supervisors' ratings of students' effectiveness with their clients?

6. Is there a relationship between students' levels of
ego development and the content of their perceptions of
their clients?

Definition of Terms

Ego development refers to the central concept of personality in Loevinger's (1966, 1976; Loevinger & Wessler,
1970) developmental stage theory which is marked by increasing differentiation and integration of perceptions, a shift

from an external to an internal focus, and complimentary changes in interpersonal behaviors.

Level of ego development refers to one of the ten stages or transitional levels in the stage theory and is measured in this study by scores on the Sentence Completion Test (SCT) (Loevinger & Wessler, 1970; Loevinger, Wessler, & Redmore, 1970).

Level of cognitive complexity refers to the degree of differentiation in a person's perceptions or constructs as defined by Kelly (1955) and Landfield (1977). It is measured in this study by Differentiation (FIC) scores on the Repertory Grid Technique (Fransella & Bannister, 1977).

Level of cognitive integration refers to the hierarchial arrangement of a person's perceptions or constructs as defined by Kelly (1955) and Landfield (1977). It is measured in this study by Ordination scores on the Repertory Grid Technique (Fransella & Bannister, 1977).

Level of meaningfulness refers to the degree of polarization of the perceptions or constructs a person uses to describe self or others, as defined by Kelly (1955) and Landfield (1977). It is measured in this study by Extremity scores on the Repertory Grid Technique (Fransella & Bannister, 1977).

Behavior with clients refers to the counselors' in-session interactions with clients, including levels of warmth, emotional involvement, positive attitudes, and attempts to examine clients' underlying psychodynamics. It is measured in this study by scores on the Vanderbilt Psychotherapy Process Scales (VPPS) (O'Malley, Suh, & Strupp, 1983; Strupp, 1981).

Effectiveness with clients refers to counselors' performance during supervision and counseling sessions and includes behavior, knowledge, and attitude. It is measured in this study by individual supervisors' ratings of counselors' effectiveness on the Counselor Evaluation Rating Scale (CERS) (Myrick & Kelly, 1971).

Content of perceptions refers to four categories of counselors' perceptions of their clients (i.e., physical characteristics or factual information, interactional style, roles or habitual activities, psychological or cognitive attributes). It is measured in this study by a classification system devised by Duck (1973).

Level of experience refers to the amount of training the supervisee has completed, i.e., registration for a first practicum, second practicum, or internship experience.

Overview of Remaining Chapters

Relevant theoretical literature and empirical research is reviewed in Chapter II. The methodology used in the study is described in Chapter III. Descriptive data and results of the statistical analyses are presented in Chapter IV. Discussion of the results, implications, and conclusions are covered in Chapter V.

CHAPTER II
REVIEW OF THE LITERATURE

Chapter II describes the current developmental models
of supervision education and reviews research investigating
the dimensions of the developmental models, including related
literature exploring individual differences between supervisees affecting their learning and performance. The chapter also describes the theory of ego development and its
stages, reviews validation research of its theoretical assumptions, and compares and contrasts ego development with
other developmental theories relevant to counselor development and supervision education.

Supervision Education

Supervision has frequently been conceptualized as an
educational process by which supervisors continue to "teach"
counseling to their supervisees. Theorists and researchers
have offered varied explanations for how students learn to
become counselors and how supervisors function as educators
in the learning process. Leddick and Bernard's (1980)
historical review of dynamic, facilitative, and behavioral
supervision theories, for example, reveals a consistent
view of the supervisor as educator. Other authors have
discussed supervision in terms of the roles or functions of

the supervisor, including teaching, counseling, and consulting (Bernard, 1979; Boyd, 1978, Gurk & Wicas, 1979; Hess,
1980b; Littrell et al., 1979). Hart (1982) has grouped
numerous supervision approaches into three categories:
skill development (supervisor as teacher), personal growth
(supervisor as counselor), and integrative (supervisor as
consultant) models. He also discusses four goals specific
to supervision's educative function: clinical knowledge and
skills, professional identity, case conceptualization, and
self-awareness. Other writers have described how supervisors with different theoretical orientations to counseling
facilitate counselors' learning of skills and/or qualities
specified by the counseling theory (for example, see
Bartlett et al., 1983; Hess, 1980a). Thus, whatever the role
described for the supervisor by theorists, the goal of
supervision has been an educational one: promoting student
learning in one or more areas such as counseling skills,
self-awareness, or counselor-client interactions.

These supervision theories have been criticized, however, for being primarily adjuncts to counseling theories
rather than distinct theories of supervision education
(Bartlett, 1983), for being "metaphors of experience" rather
than scientifically established theories (Holloway &
Hosford, 1983, p 75). This view has led some reviewers of
supervision literature to conclude there is a lack of a
theoretical base for supervision education (Holloway &
Hosford, 1983, Leddick & Bernard, 1980; Mahon & Altmann,

1977). Jolloway and Hosford (1983), however, have noted
that recent developmental models of supervision do not
equate the counseling and supervision processes and relationships but differentiate "between the process of counseling and the process of becoming a counselor" (p. 73)
They believe these developmental models offer a framework
for a systematic approach to research which can provide the
empirical evidence for a sound theory of supervision education.

Developmental Models of Supervision Education

The developmental models of supervision education are
based in the work of cognitive-developmental stage theorists
such as Hunt (conceptual systems), Kohlberg (moral judgment),
Loevinger (ego development), and Perry (intellectual-ethical
development). The movement toward cognitive-developmental
theories has been described as a "genuine advance" in understanding personality development and individual differences
(Loevinger & Knoll, 1983). Swenson (1977, 1980b) believes
the study of cognitive processes will provide a general
paradigm for psychology and a single framework for psychotherapy. Miller and Parker (in Kohlberg & Wasserman, 1930)
describe the cognitive-developmental approach as a "paradigm
shift" in counseling and guidance; they invited major
theorists to speak at a special conference on the implications for the field in 1977.

The recent descriptions of supervision as a developmental process highlight the educational nature of supervision. These models describe counselor growth as a series of sequential, hierarchial stages, each of which requires different supervision instructional strategies. The four predominant developmental models vary in their base for describing the stages: Littrell et al. (1979) focus on the roles of functions of the supervisor; Loganbill, Hardy, and Delworth (1982), the dynamics of the supervisee; Blocher (1983) and Stoltenberg (1981), the dynamics of the learning process.

The developmental framework presented by Littrell et al. (1979) focuses on the changing roles or behaviors of the supervisor in responding to the supervisee's stage of development. The authors suggest supervision moves through four stages characterized primarily by the changing tasks of the supervisor· establishing a working relationship, goals and contract; counseling and/or teaching models; consulting model; self-supervision model. Supervisees gradually assume greater responsibility for their learning, so that in the final self-supervision stage the supervisee conceptualizes, implements, controls, and manages supervision. The model of Littrell et al. thus describes changing roles, responsibilities, and behaviors of the supervisor and supervisee rather than changes in the supervisee as a person.

In their developmental model, Loganbill et al. (1982) focus instead on the dynamics of supervisees. They propose

supervisees confront a series of eight "supervisory issues"
(i.e., competence, emotional awareness, autonomy, theoretical identity, respect for individual differences, purpose
and direction, personal motivation, professional ethics)
based on Chickering's developmental tasks of college students. The authors view counselor development as continuous
and on-going, with counselors recycling through these issues
by stages of stagnation, confusion, and integration. They
suggest supervisors use facilitative, confrontive, conceptual, prescriptive, and catalytic interventions to facilitate counselor growth through the stages. Because of
individual differences (not specified by the authors),
counselors may function at different competency levels for
each developmental issue. The Loganbill et al. model does
not propose an overall stage sequence, and it does not offer a theoretical basis (i.e., personality theory) to
explain how changes occur.

In contrast, Blocher's (1983) cognitive-developmental
approach to supervision draws from theories of the psychology
of learning (e.g., Lanning, Kell and Mueller, Strong,
Krumboltz) and cognitive development (e.g., Piaget,
Loevinger, Kohlberg, Perry, Harvey, Hunt and Schroder). He
defines supervision as "a specialized instructional process
in which the supervisor attempts to facilitate the growth
of a counselor-in-preparation, using as the primary educational medium the student's interaction with real clients
for whose welfare this student has some degree of

professional, ethical, and moral responsibility" (p. 27)
This specialized instruction is "psychological education in
the fullest and most complete sense of the term" (p. 28).

Blocher's (1983) cognitive-developmental approach to
supervision education is designed to encourage cognitive
growth of a counselor toward more complex, comprehensive,
and integrative thinking. Growth in the cognitive schemas
used for information-processing of human interaction is
viewed as a prerequisite for changes in feelings and behaviors. Higher order cognitive schemas are encouraged through
a developmental learning environment balancing challenge and
support, innovation and integration. Blocher believes one
strength of his model is its capacity to adjust to students'
individual differences in learning styles and current developmental stage. The model as presented does not specify
these adjustments or developmental stages of growth but
focuses on the dynamics of the learning environment which
will promote counselor cognitive growth.

Stoltenberg (1981) describes a developmental model
which combines supervision and instructional theories and
highlights the supervisor-supervisee relationship. His
model integrates Hogan's (1964) concise four-level developmental model of supervision and Hunt's (1971) levels of conceptual development, and then applies Hunt and Sullivan's
(1974) person-environment matching approach to instruction.
The resulting "counselor complexity model" is a description
of cognitive and personality characteristics of counselors

at each of the four levels and optimal matching learning
environments for supervision at each level. The focus of
the levels is on the issues of dependency and autonomy,
describing counselors as moving from a beginning level
characterized by dependency on the supervisor (Level 1)
through successive levels of dependency-autonomy conflict
(Level II), conditional dependency (Level III), to a will-
fully interdependent master counselor (Level IV). Optimal
learning environments are matched to the developmental needs
of counselors at each level and are designed to facilitate
a counselor's advancement to the next stage. These supervision environments are characterized by a decrease in the
structure and instruction provided by the supervisor, and
an increase in a peer-like, collegial relationship between
counselor and supervisor.

Stoltenberg (1981) specifies "no specific time table
of progress" (p. 60) and does not tie his developmental
levels to experience levels exclusively. His model thus
recognizes "the different motivations, needs, and potential
resistances of counselors at different levels or stages of
development" (p. 59). He states that development will vary
"significantly from trainee to trainee" (p. 60), depending
"on the skills and attributes of the trainee" (p. 63).

Stoltenberg (1981) delineates four factors a supervisor
should consider as a basis for discriminating between counselors as unique persons and choosing appropriate interventions: the counselor's cognitive, motivational, value,

and sensory orientations. While the latter is more descriptive of the counselor's learning style and so is more directly applicable to choice of supervision instructional mode, the first three orientations address relevant cognitive and personal characteristics. A counselor's cognitive, motivational, and value orientations are three variables which may explain in part the individual variations in counselor development this model assumes. Stoltenberg urges "a further delineation of the characteristics of counselors at different levels" (p. 64) which can better indicate appropriate choices of supervision learning environments and can serve as a basis for future studies evaluating the effectiveness of different supervision techniques. He concludes, "Once this task has been accomplished for all levels of counselor trainees, the factors appearing to be most instrumental in effecting change during the supervision process can be operationalized and subjected to empirical scrutiny" (p. 64).

Miller (1982) has made a similar point. He has criticized developmental models of supervision for their lack of attention to the psychological processes evolving in counselors during development. He calls attention to three underlying processes (i.e., conceptual and ego development, emotional flexibility and congruence, awareness) which he believes are crucial to understanding and facilitating counselor growth. In reviews of supervision research, Holloway and Hosford (1983) and Lambert (1980) have called attention to the need for descriptive, exploratory studies to identify relevant supervisee variables, effective supervision techniques, and desired supervision outcomes.

In summary, while developmental models of supervision education vary in their central focus (i.e., supervisors' roles, supervisee dynamics, learning process), each describes a common thread of counselor development. Counselors are assumed to have different supervision needs, be concerned with different issues about counseling, and have different levels of self-awareness at various stages of development. Most developmental models assume counselor development depends not only on counseling experience level, but more importantly on individual differences or personal attributes of the counselors themselves. Although the developmental models emphasize individual differences, delineating what the relevant differences are is an incomplete task at present (Miller, 1983; Stoltenberg, 1981).

Research Related to Developmental Models of Supervision Education

Few published studies to date have been tied directly to a particular developmental model. In addition, most supervision-related research has primarily used beginning practicum students (Hart, 1982; Holloway & Hosford, 1983; Lambert, 1980) and investigated the acquisition of basic counseling skills (Lambert, 1980), so that little is known empirically about supervision of counselors at advanced

levels of training (Lambert, 1980)   Some cross-sectional
and longitudinal studies have addressed issues relevant to
developmental models. Most have investigated counselors'
preferences for or perceptions of supervision; only a few
have identified developmental changes in behaviors of counselors at different levels of experience (Reising & Daniels,
1983). Like the developmental theorists, these research
studies often point to the need to attend to individual
differences of counselors.

A recent study based on Stoltenberg's model (Miars,
Tracey, Ray, Cornfeld, O'Farrell, & Gelso, 1983) found supervisors perceived themselves varying their behaviors with
supervisees at different experience levels. They perceived
themselves offering inexperienced supervisees (first or
second semester practicum) more structure, direction, support, and teaching, while emphasizing personal development,
client resistance, and transference/countertransference
issues with more experienced supervisees (advanced practicum or intern level). The authors concluded the supervisors
were clearly "making some kind of developmental distinctions
when describing the nature of their supervision across
various trainee levels" (p. 410). Even though the variations closely paralleled the optimal supervision educational
environments proposed by Stoltenberg (1981), the authors
could not specify from their data what distinctions the
supervisors were using to make decisions about their supervisory behavior. The supervisors also seemed to make more

"gross developmental distinctions" (p. 410) (two levels)
than those postulated by Stoltenberg (four levels).

Counselors' views of supervision across experience levels

Counselors at various levels of experience have also
reported different perceptions of or preferences for supervision.

Littrell (1978), for example, factor analyzed the concerns of beginning counselors. He found the prepracticum
counselors most concerned about learning techniques and
meeting client needs, moderately concerned about the counselor role and adequacy, and least concerned about whether
clients like them.

Worthington and Roehlke (1979) investigated beginning
counselors' perceptions of effective supervision. First
practicum counselors indicated they preferred direct teaching (i.e., modeling, feedback, literature) within a supportive relationship. They felt they had improved their
counseling as a result of these qualities in addition to
supervisors' support and encouragement of risking new
behaviors and to develop their own styles. They described
competent supervisors as having greater experience, skill,
and self-assurance

Worthington (1984) conducted a similar study of counselors at five experience levels from several geographical
areas using a cross-sectional approach. The supervisory
behaviors related to satisfaction with supervision and

perceived competence of the supervisor were the same behaviors identified by the beginning counselors in the previous study. There were some differences between experience levels, such as the more frequent focus on content with less experienced supervisees, more frequent use of consultation with internship supervisees, and more frequent encouragement to find their own style of counseling with more experienced supervisees.

Heppner and Roehlke (1984) used the same supervisory questionnaire (see Worthington & Roehlke, 1979) with beginning practica, advanced practica, and internship students, and reported similar differences by experience level for ratings of supervisory behavior which correlated with students' satisfaction. They also examined the critical incidents or turning points (classifed by the supervisory issues of Loganbill et al., 1982) reported by students at each of the three experience levels. These findings paralleled the differences in preferences for supervisory behaviors. Beginning and advanced practica students described critical incidents related to self-awareness issues; internship students, those related to personal issues affecting therapy.

Moskowitz (1981) compared supervision preferences of counselors at several experience levels. Beginning clinical psychology students preferred an imitative approach, emphasizing learning techniques and role modeling, while more advanced students preferred a therapist-centered approach, emphasizing exploration and attention to therapist role

difficulties. Beginning students also indicated a preference
for more direction and less focus on errors than advanced
students. Nash's (1975) results suggested similar sequential differences, with students moving from a preference for
advice, technical suggestions, and support to a preference
for more discussion of theoretical and countertransference
issues. In related literature, a review of teacher education research indicated a similar pattern: student teachers'
preferences for directive supervision decreased over time
while experienced teachers consistently preferred nondirec-
tive supervision (Copeland, 1982).

Cross and Brown (1983) found counselors at different
experience levels also perceived their supervisors behaving
differently Counselors indicated the frequency of their
supervisors' behaviors on Worthington and Roehlke's (1979)
list. Beginning counselors perceived their supervisors
emphasized tasks and methods (i.e., observations, audiotapes), while more experienced counselors perceived their
supervisors emphasized both a more supportive and more
intense relationship. The latter indicated they received
more confrontation and feedback, saw their supervisors as
more competent, and said supervision contributed more to
improved client outcome and increased counselor self-
confidence than did the beginning counselors.

In post-hoc interviews of a longitudinal study, counselors reported similar changes in their relationships with
their supervisors, moving from dependency and anxiety about

the supervisor's judgments and evaluations to a more peer-like, consultative relationship (Hill, Charles, & Reed, 1981)

Counselors' behaviors across experience levels

Other studies have identified developmental changes in behaviors of counselors at different levels of experience. Cicchetti and Ornston (1976) reported a series of studies analyzing the structure and content of responses of novice and experienced psychotherapists. Novices asked more questions during an initial interview, but with training the number of questions they asked was not different from experienced psychotherapists. Content analysis of responses to a filmed client revealed significant differences between the two groups, with novices using more concrete statements while experienced psychotherapists used more abstract comments which did not focus on the exact words or actions of the client. The experienced psychotherapists' responses instead seemed to attempt an integrated understanding of the client's messages about self.

Hill et al. (1981) conducted a three-year longitudinal study of twelve counseling psychology students and found changes in their verbal responses in brief counseling sessions with volunteer clients. The students used more minimal encouragers (i.e., simple agreement or understanding) but fewer questions (open and closed) over time. No differences were found for the use of directives (i.e.,

information, direct guidance) and results for the use of
complex responses (i.e., interpretation, confrontation) were
inconsistent, perhaps a result of the brevity of the counseling session, the researchers concluded. In post-hoc
interviews, the students reported they felt they had improved most in higher order skills such as timing, appro-
priateness of intervention, client dynamics, and techniques
for special populations.

These studies provide some support for a developmental
model of supervision; both supervisees and supervisors report
and/or evidence changes over time. Other studies, however,
have pointed to the effect of individual differences of
counselors as mediating variables for level of experience,
an effect assumed in several developmental models (i.e.,
Blocher, 1983; Loganbill et al., 1982; Stoltenberg, 1981).

Individual counselor variation

The confounding effects of individual differences have
been illustrated by Reising and Daniels' (1983) attempt to
validate Hogan's (1964) developmental model. Practicum,
advanced practicum students, interns, and professional
staff rated statements they might make about themselves
(e.g., "I lack the experience to know what to do with my
clients") and statements they might make about their supervision needs (e.g., "I need a supervisor who will be confrontive with me"). The statements were designed to reflect
issues in the first three levels of Hogan's model. A factor

analysis revealed less experienced trainees were in general more anxious, dependent, and technique-oriented, and less ready for confrontation, while more experienced counselors were more independent, as the·theory described. The professional staff, however, also reported more commitment ambivalence, contrary to expectations based on Hogan's model. They identified doubts about their own skill and the helpfulness of counseling. While the respondents' response patterns supported Hogan's model of counselor development in general, the authors concluded that a simple stage model could not adequately describe the complexity of the issues hogan included. They added, "supervisors may need to go beyond the simple developmental model and examine how the complex model's individual issues are organized within each trainee" (p. 242).

Grayson (1979) reported tolerance of ambiguity related more strongly to counselors' preferences for supervision than experience level. For counselors ranging from no practicum experience to those in their second year of internship, higher levels of tolerance of ambiguity correlated with a preference for experiential supervision; low levels of tolerance, with didactic supervision.

In addition, Friedlander and Snyder (1983) included self-efficacy expectations of counselors at various experience levels in a study of outcome expectancies of supervision and expectations of supervisor's attributes and role. High levels of confidence and high levels of expectations that supervision would affect clients predicted high expectations for expert and evaluative supervisors; level of experience, however, was not predictive of expectations. Like Reising and Daniels (1983), the authors concluded "individual differences override level of experience" (p. 348).

Counselor skill acquisition. The need to attend to individual differences has also been of concern to reviewers of research on skill acquisition who have cited the need to investigate the impact of counselors' personal attributes on the learning process (Bartlett, 1983, Holloway & Hosford, 1983; Lambert, 1930; Mahon & Altmann, 1977). Counseling students' cognitive complexity, for example, has been shown to affect their learning. Rosenthal (1977) investigated the effect of first semester counseling students' conceptual level on learning confrontation skills taught by two approaches. Self-instruction materials were more effective with high conceptual level students, while guided instruction was more effective with low level students. Rosenthal concluded counselor educators needed to consider the possible interactions of students' personality characteristics with training approaches.

Reviewers have also cited research suggesting counselor-trainees neither retain nor transfer skills to other settings (Lambert, 1980; Leddick & Bernard, 1980; Mahon & Altmann, 1977). Spooner and Stone (1977), for example, evaluated

tapes of student counselors during prepracticum, practicum,
and three months after training In the follow-up tapes,
students used less confrontation and goal setting, considered more advanced skills, and used more questions,
considered a basic skill.

Mahon and Altmann (1977) have concluded individual
variables may influence the effects of training more than
a specific training procedure. They recall that Rogers'
core conditions describe feelings and attitudes of the
helper, not the specific skills operationalized from these
qualities by Truax and Carkhuff and others. "Personal
qualities underlying and unifying 'skills' need as much or
more emphasis as the skills themselves" (p. 49), they
added. This conclusion echoes statements made by developmental theorists (i.e., Blocher, 1983; Miller, 1982,
Loganbill et al., 1982; Stoltenberg, 1981) and reviewers of
supervision research (Holloway & Hosford, 1983; Lambert,
1980) who have also cited the need to attend to individual
differences of counselors

Sources of individual counselor variation. Mahon and
Altmann (1977) proposed counselor educators use the tenets
of perceptual psychology and the "self as instrument" concept (Combs, 1969), a concept which might explain individual
differences in counselors. They believe perceptions underlying behaviors--beliefs, attitudes, and values--are the
integrating learning forces. "It is not the skills themselves which are all important, it is the control of their

use, the <u>intentions</u> with which they are used, and their
<u>flexibility</u> or changeability that is so crucial" (p. 49),
they explained. According to this view, changes in perceptions would be necessary for changes in behavior to be
real and long-lasting, and more and less effective counselors
would be expected to differ in their perceptions of self,
others, and the helping process. Such perceptual differences
have been found in research of counselors, teachers, and
pastors using an instrument based on Combs' (1969) concept
(Brown, 1970; Combs, 1969; Dedrick, 1972; Rotter, 1972;
Vonk, 1970). Other studies using measures of cognitive
complexity, a concept which in part reflects the degree of
perceptual flexibility, have found similar differences
between more and less complex counselors' verbal responses
to clients (Goldberg, 1974; Lichtenberg & Heck, 1979) and
their empathy skills (Heck & Davis, 1973; Lutwak &
Hennessy, 1982).

Research of counselor attitudes, a possible source of
individual differences, has also illustrated the impact of
counselors' perceptions of others. For example, stereo-
typing has been found to interfere with counselors' processing of information about ethnic minority clients (Wampold,
Casas, & Atkinson, 1981) and homosexual versus heterosexual
individuals (Casas, Brady, & Ponterotto, 1983). In addition, Hirsch and Stone (1982) found trainee's attitudes
toward a particular counseling skill affected performance
of that skill. After brief training, student volunteers

with positive attitudes toward reflection of feeling gave
higher quality reflections to coached clients than volunteers with negative attitudes. Such a relationship was not
found for interpretive responses, however.

Studies of personality traits which might explain
individual differences in counselor effectiveness have pro-
duced mixed results (Kaplan, 1983). These studies used
global measures of personality, such as the California
Personality Inventory, Omnibus Personality Inventory, and
the 16 PF, and correlated them with overall effectiveness
ratings made by clients or supervisors. Effective counseling students had those general qualities expected in good
counselors; they were more introspective, esthetically
sensitive, emotionally expressive, flexible, tolerant, independent, and capable of intimate relationships. Much like
Mahon and Altmann (1977), Kaplan (1983) concluded, "Overall
the research on personality attributes supports the notion
that it is not what trainees possess that is important, but
rather how they use it in interacting with the client"
(p. 223).

Conclusion

The need to attend to individual differences and personal attributes of counselors has thus been a theme in
developmental models of supervision and critiques of them,
in research classifying students by experience level, in
related research of counselors' skill acquisition, and in

research on counselors' personal attributes. Developmental theorists, researchers, and reviewers of supervision research believe an awareness of counselors' personal attributes will enhance a supervisor's understanding of counselor learning and choosing interventions for more effective supervision education. Research studies have found both supervisors and counselors believe supervisors vary their behaviors but have not identified what criteria other than counselors' experience level supervisors may be using to make their decisions about those behaviors. The individual personal attributes which would be critical for supervisors to consider has not been specified in a detailed, comprehensive developmental model by either theorists or researchers.

Lambert (1980) and Holloway and Hosford (1983) have called for such a "prescriptive model" of supervision education, one which would "predict what types of supervision techniques will result in what types of trainee outcomes for which type of trainee" (Holloway & Hosford, 1983, p. 75). They also cite the need to delineate the desired outcomes of supervision, especially for the advanced student, who has seldom been included in supervision research. It seems ironic that while supervision has been identified as a central, significant learning experience during a counseling program by both educators (Banikiotes, 1977; Lambert, 1980) and students (Hart, 1982; Hill et al., 1981), we have conducted supervision without a clear knowledge of the critical

variables impacting learning or the goals and desired outcomes of the learning process.

Holloway and Hosford (1983) believe developmental
models provide the starting point for building a prescriptive theory. They cite the need for exploratory, descriptive studies to identify critical variables which can then
be studied in experimental research designs.

Ego Development

The concept of ego development and the theory of ego
development stages (Loevinger, 1966, 1976; Loevinger &
Wessler, 1970) seem to provide a framework sophisticated
and complex enough to serve as a basis for a model of
counselor development. Loevinger refers to ego development
as the "master trait" or "central core of personality"
(Loevinger & Knoll, 1983), second only to intelligence in
explaining human variability (Loevinger, 1966). Ego development reflects a "person's frame of reference" (Loevinger,
1979, p 284) or describes "the framework of meaning which
one subjectively imposes on experience" (Hauser, 1976, p.
930).

Levels of ego development describe a "sequence from
egocentric impulsivity, through rule-bound conformity, to
a self-aware orientation that fulfills its self-chosen
responsibilities, to value for individuality and acceptance
of inner conflict" (Loevinger & Knoll, 1983, p. 202) Ten
stages and transitional levels mark this progression, as
described in Table 2.

TABLE 1

SOME MILESTONES OF EGO DEVELOPMENT

Stage	Impulse Control Character Development	Interpersonal Style	Conscious Preoccupations	Cognitive Style
Presocial Symbiotic		Autistic Symbiotic	Self vs. non-self	
Impulsive	Impulsive, fear of retaliation	Receiving, dependent, exploitive	Bodily feelings, especially sexual and aggressive	Stereotype, conceptual confusion
Self-protective	Fear of being caught, externalizing blame, opportunistic	Wary, manipulative, exploitive	Self-protection, wishes, things, advantage, control	
Conformist	Conformity to external rules, shame, guilt for breaking rules	Belonging, helping, superficial niceness	Appearance, social acceptability, banal feelings, behavior	Conceptual simplicity, stereotypes, cliches
Conscientious	Self-evaluated standards, self-criticism, guilt for consequences, long-term goals	Intensive, responsible, mutual, concern for communication	Differentiated feelings, motives for behavior, self-respect, achievements, traits, expression	Conceptual complexity, idea of patterning
Autonomous	Add: Coping with conflicting inner needs, toleration	Add: Respect for autonomy	Vividly conveyed feelings, integration of physiological and psychological, psychological causation of behavior, development, role conception, self-fulfillment, self in social context	Increased conceptual complexity, complex patterns, toleration for ambiguity, broad scope, objectivity
Integrated	Add: Reconciling inner conflicts, renunciation of unattainable	Add: Cherish individuality	Add: Identity	

NOTE: "Add" means in addition to the description applying to the previous level.

Note. Source: Loevinger & Wessler, 1970, pp. 10-11. Reprinted by permission of the publisher.

Relevance to Counseling and Counselor Development

Loevinger's (Loevinger & Wessler, 1970) descriptions of ego development stages illustrate how persons, and therefore counselors, at each level perceive others and interact with them. At the Impulsive (I-2) stage, "people are seen as sources of supply" (Loevinger & Wessler, 1970, p. 57); at the Self-protective (Delta) stage, people are viewed as either taking advantage of oneself or as able to be manipulated and exploited; at the Conformist (I-3) stage, people are described in stereotypic, conventional terms (especially sex roles); at the Self-aware (I-3/4) transition stage, basic individual differences are acknowledged; at the Conscientious (I-4) stage, interpersonal relations are described in terms of mutuality; at the Individualistic (I-4/5) transition stage, interpersonal relations are viewed as a process, changing over time and having interactive effects; at the Autonomous (I-5) stage, each person's individuality and uniqueness is cherished; at the Integrated (I-6) stage, identity and self-fulfillment for self and others is respected.

Besides the changes in relationships, Loevinger also describes other aspects of ego development particularly germane to counseling (Loevinger & Wessler, 1970). For instance, at the Conscientious (I-4) level, a person is able to identify underlying feelings and patterns of behavior, and is beginning to formulate explanations in terms of psychological causality. The Individualistic (I-4/5) person distinguishes between process and outcome, inner and outer life, appearance and reality. The Autonomous (I-5) person has a high tolerance for ambiguity and sees complex and circular forces in interpersonal relationships, and is concerned with broad social issues. The Integrated (I-6) person additionally understands paradox and thus is able to transcend and reconcile conflicts.

In addition, Loevinger (1976) has outlined the similarities and parallels of the stages of ego development and the stages of the process of therapy as described by Rogers (1961) (see Table 3). For example, the Self-protective (Delta) person perceives problems as external and has no sense of personal responsibility for them. Stage progression is marked by increased recognition and expression of concern about contradictions between experience and self, and increased acceptance of responsibility for problems. The Autonomous (I-5) person owns changing feelings and trusts the process of evolving and reformulating perceptions of self and others. The Integrated (I-6) person resembles Maslow's self-actualizing person (Loevinger, 1979).

In support of the parallel developmental sequences of ego development and therapy, Atkins (1976, and in Loevinger, 1979) found female clients' perceptions of counseling were related to their ego levels. When asked to discuss a problem related to being a woman, pre-Conscientious (I-4) female clients focused on control of emotions and concrete aspects

44

TABLE 3

COMPARISON OF EGO DEVELOPMENT STAGES AND ROGERS' PROCESS OF THERAPY STAGES

Stage	Ego Development — Description	Process of Psychotherapy — Description	Stage
I-2	S tends to dichotomize the world, stereotyping is the most conspicuous sign	Personal constructs are rigid	1
	Affects are seen as bodily states or impulses rather than as differentiated inner feelings	Feelings and personal meanings are not recognized or owned Communication is about externals only	
	There is a limited emotional range		
	Trouble is located in a place rather than a situation	No problems are recognized or perceived, there is no desire to change	
Δ	S does not see himself as responsible for trouble or failure, you are lucky or unlucky, or other people are to blame or blame is external and impersonal	Problems are perceived as external to self S has no sense of personal responsibility for problems	2
Δ/3	Obedience and conformity to norms are simple absolute rules	Personal constructs are rigid and thought of as facts, not recognized as constructs	
I-3	Inner life is measured in generalities, feelings are deemed or mentioned in vague, evasive, or non-committal way	Differentiation of personal meanings and feelings is limited and global	
	Inner conflict may be manifest, but it is not acknowledged	Contradictions may be expressed but without recognition as contradictions	
I-3/4	Self consciousness and individuality self awareness and self criticism are characteristic	There is freer flow of expression about self self related experiences and self is reflected in others	3
	There is stronger awareness of feelings than before S is more aware of individual differences in attitudes, interests, and abilities but still in global and banal terms	Differentiation of feelings and meanings is slightly sharper and less global than before	
	S sees multiple possibilities and alternatives in situations, there are contingencies, exceptions, and comparisons, though global and banal ones	There is recognition of contradictions in experience	
I-4	S has a richly differentiated inner life, experiences are savored and appreciated	Free feelings as described is intense, present feelings are still distrusted and feared	4
	S is aware of the problem of impulse and control		

I-4	Interpersonal interaction is intensive		5
	S sees patterns in behavior and has a vivid sense of individual differences in behavior in the long term dispositions that underlie behavior	There is increased differentiation of feelings, constructs, and personal meanings seeking exactness of symbolization	
	Descriptions of people are more realistic because S perceives more complexities		
	S is aware of self, reflects on self, and describes self and others in terms of reflexive traits. S sees intentions and motives as well as consequences of behavior	S is concerned about contradictions and incongruities between experience and self	
	S distinguishes appearances from underlying feelings		
	S has a strong sense of responsibility	There are feelings of self responsibility in problems, though such feelings vacillate	
	S sees life as presenting choices, he holds the origin of his own destiny		
I-4/5	Where the I-4 S sees polar, incompatible opposites, the I-4/5 S is more likely to see a paradox, a quasi-contradiction in nature rather than a forced choice	There is increasingly clear facing of contradictions and incongruities in experience	
	S becomes aware of conflicting or contrasting emotion	Feelings are close to being fully experienced	
	There is greater complexity in conception of interpersonal interaction. The idea of communication and expression of feelings is deepened and made more complex. Psychological causality replaces vague statements of reasons and problems. It gives vivid and personal versions of ideas presented as cliches at lower levels	There are fresh discoveries of personal constructs and a critical examination of them. There is a strong tendency towards exactness in differentiation of feelings and meanings	
		There is increased acceptance of self responsibility for problems and freer internal communication	
	S distinguishes inner life from outer, appearances from reality. Maintaining one's own individuality is perceived as a problem	There is increasing ownership of self feelings and a desire to be the "real me"	6
I-5	S feels the full force of inner conflict and tries to cope with it or transcend it	New feelings are experienced with immediacy and richness of detail	
	S is concerned with communicating feelings	Differentiation of experiencing is sharp and basic	
	Emotions are differentiated and vividly conveyed. Sensual experiences come through vividly. S displays spontaneity, genuineness, intensity	There is acceptant ownership of changing feelings, a basic trust in his own process	7
	S has a high tolerance for ambiguity, conflicting alternatives are construed as aspects of many faceted life situations	Personal constructs are tentatively formulated and loosely held	

NOTE. Descriptions of stages of ego development are excerpted from Loevinger and Wessler, 1970, Chapter Four, pp 54-109. Descriptions of stages 1 psychotherapy are excerpted from Rogers, 1961, Chapter Seven, pp 125-159

Note. Source: Loevinger, 1976, pp. 153-155
Reprinted by permission of the publisher.

of woman's role, home, family, and mother. Post-Conscientious (I-4) females were concerned with relationship, abstract aspects of woman's role, self-identity, and independence. The two groups also differed in their conceptions
of the purpose of psychotherapy. Low ego level women
stressed working out solutions; realizing, alleviating, and
coping with feelings; and adjusting to society. High ego
level women emphasized self-understanding; the self as
hidden or internally blocked; the relationship between
therapist and patient; patterns of behavior and being stuck
in them; and connections between thoughts, feelings, and
actions

Higher levels of ego development should not be equated
with better adjustment, however; they do not represent a
"conflict-free sphere" (Loevinger, 1966, p. 205). Loevinger
explains, "Every stage has its weaknesses, its problems,
and its paradoxes, which provide both a potential for mal-
adjustment and potential for growth" (p. 200).

Counselor educators' views of ego development

Several counselor education theorists have highlighted
ego development theory's relevance to counseling and counselor development (Blocher, 1983; Miller, 1982; Swenson,
1977, 1980a,b). Swenson (1977), for example, describes ego
development as "the central personality variable in interpersonal relations" (p. 41) and concludes it seems the most
applicable to counseling of the current general developmental

theories (Swenson, 1980b). He believes it provides a basis
for organizing, relating, and selecting appropriate theoretical interventions for clients at different ego levels
(Swenson, 1977, 1980b) and has implications for optimum
levels of ego functioning for counselors (Swenson, 1980b).
What would be the effects of differences between counselor
and client ego levels, he asks and theorizes counselors
might function better in settings where the counseling work
"matches" their ego functioning.

Both Miller (1982) and Blocher (1983) specify Loevinger
as one of the stage theorists who serve as the bases for
their developmental approaches to supervision. Miller
(1982), for example, cites Loevinger's theory when he discusses conceptual and ego development, but the descriptions
of his other two processes (emotional flexibility and congruence, and awareness) also reflect dimensions incorporated
into Loevinger's theory. For instance, his awareness continuum (unawareness, denial, suppression, awareness, integration) closely parallels the development of awareness
described by Loevinger's stages of ego development. His
final two stages, autonomous and integrated, have the same
names as Loevinger's stages.

Blocher's (1983) description of the counselor at a high
level of cognitive functioning, the goal of his approach,
closely parallels Loevinger's description of the person at
the Integrated (I-6) level of ego development:

This functioning includes the ability to take multiple perspectives in order to achieve empathic understanding with people who hold a variety of world views, value systems and personal constructs. It includes the ability to differentiate among and manipulate a wide range and large number of relevant facts and causal factors. Finally, it involves the ability to integrate and synthesize in creative or unusual ways large amounts of such information to arrive at an understanding of the psychological identity and life situation of a wide range of other human beings. Still further the counselor engages in this quest in active collaboration with the client, and in the hope of imparting some skill and understanding of the process to the client. (Blocher, 1983, p. 28)

While Blocher (1983) details the behavior of the supervisor who seeks to educate a counselor with these abilities and qualities, he does not include a description of sequential changes in counselor's perceptions and behaviors during this educational process. Instead he directs the supervisor to the stage theorists he uses as bases for his model: Piaget and Inhelder, Loevinger, Kohlberg, Perry, and Harvey, Hunt and Schroder.

Stoltenberg's (1981) descriptions of counselor characteristics at his four levels of development often suggest ego development stages, although he does not specify Loevinger as a source. For example, the Level I counselor, unilaterally dependent on the supervisor, lacking self-awareness, is "quite concerned with rules of counseling" and "searching for the right way to do things" (p. 61), much like the Conformist (I-3) person. The more empathic and tolerant Level III counselor exhibits a more highly differentiated interpersonal style, and acknowledges individual

differences, as Individualistic (I-4/5) and Autonomous (I-5)
persons do.

Research Support for Ego Development

Loevinger has integrated the theories of Piaget,
Sullivan, Erikson, Fromm, Kohlberg, Perry, and Harvey, Hunt,
and Sullivan (Loevinger, 1976; Loevinger & Wessler, 1970)
into a common thread of development. As a result the
theory of ego development has empirical support from the
work of psychoanalysts, sociologists, philosophers, and
psychologists represented in its integration (Loevinger,
1976).

To measure ego development, Loevinger and her associ-
ates at the Social Science Institute at Washington University
have created a sentence completion test and have conducted
on-going research to refine the items and the detailed
scoring manual. Studies of the validity of theoretical
assumptions of ego development have all used the Sentence
Completion Test (SCT) (Loevinger & Wessler, 1970; Loevinger,
Wessler, & Redmore, 1970) (see the Instruments section of
Chapter III for a description of the test).

Unitary dimension

Evidence for the unitary dimension of ego development
and the SCT is based in a principal components analysis
which yielded an eigenvalue of 8.8 for the first principal
component and 1.2 for the second (Loevinger & Wessler, 1970).

In addition, Lambert (in Loevinger, 1979) found no subset
of moral items on the SCT in correlation with Kohlberg's
test of moral maturity, and Blasi (in Loevinger, 1979)
found no subset of responsibility items.

Polar and milestone traits

Manifestations of levels of ego development include
both polar and milestone traits (Loevinger, 1966). Polar
characteristics exhibit a linear pattern, such as the constant decrease in the tendency to categorize according to
stereotypes, while milestone sequences "tend to rise and
then fall off in prominence as one ascends the scale of ego
maturity" (Loevinger, 1966, p. 202). Research assuming a
linear relationship between ego development and some external criteria has sometimes ignored the important milestone concept and a more probable curvilinear or nonmonotonic relationship (Hauser, 1976). Hoppe and Loevinger
(1977) found an expected nonmonotonic relationship between
level of ego development and conforming behaviors, illus-
trating a milestone sequence. Expected correlations of
ego development with other traits may be positive, negative,
or curvilinear, depending on the peak stage for a particular trait (Loevinger, 1979).

Bochini (1978), for example, reported decreasing scores
on self-centered values but increasing scores on other-
centered and relational values as ego level increased.
Lasker (1978, and in Loevinger, 1979) found the need for

achievement peaked at the Conscientious (I-4) stage while
the need for power peaked at the Self-protective/Conformist
transition (Delta/3) level. In contrast, a study of the
correlation between empathy and ego level reported an expected linear relationship. Zielinski (1973) pre- and
posttested 40 graduate students in a beginning course in
counselor education on Carkhuff's index of communication of
empathy and his index of discrimination of empathic understanding. On pretest he found a moderate relationship (.46)
between level of ego development and ability to communicate
empathy, but no significant relationship with ability to
discriminate empathy. In comparisons of pre and post
scores, students with high levels of ego development gained
in ability to discriminate empathic understanding, but
neither high nor low ego level students gained in ability
to communicate empathy. Carlozzi, Gaa, and Liberman (1983)
also found differences in empathy scores for students at
different ego levels, although they did not use a correla-
tional approach but compared high and low ego levels. The
researchers administered the Affective Sensitivity Scale,
a multiple-choice measure of empathic responses to filmed
vignettes, to 51 undergraduate dormitory advisors. Undergraduates at higher levels of ego development had significantly higher empathy scores than those at lower levels.

In Rock's (1975 and in Loevinger, 1979) study of 50
undergraduate women, two measures of self-insight had highly
significant, positive linear relationships with ego

development, even with age and intelligence partialled out.
Female students at or below the Conformist (I-3) stage
tended to be unreflective or reflective in nonpsychological
terms in their own interpretations of their TAT stories and
their videotaped behavior. Most females shifted to
psychologically-minded self-reflection at the Conscientious
(I-4) stage. Almost all the females at the Individualistic
(I-4/5) and Autonomous (I-5) levels described themselves in
complex psychological terms and showed a dynamic understanding of the reasons for their behavior and inner conflicts.

Sequentiality of ego stages--deliberate psychological education

Studies reporting changes in ego level following a
theory-relevant intervention provide evidence for the sequentiality of ego development and SCT, and point to the theory's
relevance to counselor education. Researchers and educators
have devised "deliberate psychological education" curricula
in attempts to stimulate the social, personal, ego and moral
development of a variety of student populations. The programs included training in basic empathic skills and
presentations of concepts of various developmental theorists,
and they used didactic, reading, and experiential activities
and devised activities to tap into both cognitive and affective domains in students' learning. Experiential activities
usually included were devised to be practical and realistic
so that students could actually assume the role of tutor or

peer-counselor. Most of these studies have reported increases in empathic skills, moral judgment, and ego development.

The majority of these studies have used high school
students. Mosher and Sprinthall (1971), for example,
reported a one-third stage increase on Kohlberg's Moral
Judgment Scale and one full stage on Loevinger's SCT for
students in the experimental group (counseling class), but
no changes for the control group (regular psychology class).
The counseling group also gained significantly on empathy
ratings of tapes. Sullivan (1975) reported almost dupli-
cate results on moral and ego development for his control
and experimental high school groups after a one-year
curriculum.

In a study emphasizing personal growth through role
taking (Rustad & Rogers, 1975), high school students increased their moral and ego development stages and improved
their basic counseling skills. In follow-ups of a small
number of the students, the levels on all three measures
had been maintained. High school students who tutored
junior high students also increased their levels of ego
development and moral reasoning (Cognetta, 1977), as did
female high school students following a women's literature
course (Erickson, 1975, 1977b). In a junior college
psychology course which gradually decreased structure and
increased student-initiated learning, students' ego development levels increased while the reverse curriculum and
control groups showed a slight decline (Exum, 1978).

Other studies have used deliberate psychological education curricula with student teachers, counselors, and
social workers. For example, Oja and Sprinthall (1978)
taught students representing all three groups for one semester. Experimental groups did not significantly increase
their ego levels but did gain significantly on moral
thinking and cognitive complexity. They also improved
their ability to use indirect teaching methods, viewed by
the researchers as more effective than directive approaches,
and tended to become less dictatorial and arbitrary and
more empathic Hurt (1977) found that teachers who received
extensive empathy training gained significantly on measures
of ego development and moral thinking. Glassberg (1978)
used a "peer supervision" curriculum based in deliberate
psychological education principles with English education
students. The experimental group showed significant increases in ego level, moral thinking, empathic skills, and
indirect teaching skills. They also shifted from an external to a more internal locus of control.

Bernier (1980) reported on a pilot curriculum with 18
counselors and teachers in a graduate workshop in developmental education which involved classroom, prepracticum, and
field-based practicum experiences. Students showed significant pre-post increases in accurate empathy and moral
thinking, but not significant differences on conceptual
level and ego development.

Behavioral correlates of ego development

Other validation studies have focused on behavioral
correlates of ego development, although Loevinger (1979)
asserts ego levels cannot be translated into single,
specific behaviors, and so expects low correlations. In
reviews of these validation studies, Loevinger (1979) and
Hauser (1976) reported expected relationship between low ego
levels and certain behaviors   For example, adolescent boys'
conformity behaviors peaked at the Conformist (I-3) stage;
institutionalized delinquents' behaviors were negatively
correlated with ego stage; and children's behaviors reflecting responsibility were positively correlated with ego stage.
In contrast, evidence of validity for high ego levels is
based in correlations with attitudes, philosophy of life,
self-insight, and ability to communicate empathy (Loevinger,
1979).

Ego Development and Other Developmental Theories

Although other theories (i.e., Perry, Kohlberg, Harvey,
Hunt, & Schroder, and Kelly) incorporated by Loevinger into
ego development are used in counseling research and they
describe similar developmental themes and patterns,
Loevinger's theory was chosen as the theoretical basis for
this study because of its broader base and application
(Loevinger, 1976; Swenson, 1980a). The following reviews
and brief descriptions of these theories illustrate the
bases for this conclusion.

Perry

Perry's (1970) developmental scheme, based on Kohlberg's
theory of moral development, focuses on the intellectual-
ethical development of traditional age college students.
Students are theorized to move through nine major stages in
their conceptions of knowledge and values, from a simplistic,
categorical view to a complex, pluralistic one. The development scheme has been criticized because it does not en-
compass all the relevant aspects of development and has
limited applicability for other age ranges (Widick, 1977).
The scheme also lacks an established reliable and valid
assessment instrument (Widick, 1977). These criticisms
point to the developmental scheme's limited potential in
research with older graduate students.

Some counselor educators have used Perry's developmental
scheme as a theoretical basis for counseling practice and
counselor development. For example, Widick (1977) suggested the content of Perry's developmental sequence identi-
fies both goals and interventions for deliberate psychological education programs and workshops in anxiety management,
career/life planning, and peer-counselor training. Schmidt
and Davison (1983) proposed using reflective judgment, a
scheme of intellectual development extrapolated from Perry's
broader scheme, to describe important client variables and
to suggest prescriptive interventions for encouraging
client development towards greater cognitive complexity.

Cooper and Lewis (1983) used Perry's scheme to describe counseling students' typical cognitive transitions
as they try to cope with the diversity of counseling
theories. According to the authors, students move from a
dogmatic and rigid dualistic framework (i.e., right/wrong
theory), to a pragmatic acceptance of multiple theories
(i.e., whatever works), to a theoretical commitment which
recognizes the limitations of all theorizing. They also
suggested intervention strategies to facilitate students'
movement through these transitions. Researchers, however,
have not investigated the efficacy of the application of
Perry's scheme to counselor development.

Kohlberg

Loevinger and Knoll (1983) have cited Kohlberg as the
leading figure in the cognitive-developmental movement, as
both the most popular and favorite target in the field.
Kohlberg's (1969) developmental theory of moral judgment
and its stage sequence has considerable validity support
(Kohlberg & Wasserman, 1980; Loevinger & Knoll, 1983; Rest,
1980) and has been shown to be an important factor in real-
life decision-making (Rest, 1980).

Measures of moral development have correlated positively with ego development (Loevinger, 1979), and both
Kohlberg (Kohlberg & Wasserman, 1980) and Loevinger (1976)
have noted the overlap of the two theories. Studies of
deliberate psychological education have shown parallel

increases in measures of each for high school students
(Cognetta, 1977; Erickson, 1975, 1977; Mosher & Sprinthall,
1971, Rustad & Rogers, 1975; Sullivan, 1975), and teachers
(Glassberg, 1978; Hurt, 1977). Bernier (1980) reported no
increases for ego development, but significant increases in
moral judgment for counselors and teachers in a graduate
workshop.

Gilligan (1982), however, has challenged Kohlberg's
claim of universality for his stage sequence, arguing that
it only describes a masculine developmental pattern which
defines maturity in terms of autonomy and achievement and
ignores a more feminine concern with relationships. In
addition, Rest (1980) and Welfel and Lipsitz (1983b) have
identified a predominant cognitive component in moral judgment in its emphasis on the logical analysis of ethical
dilemmas. Rest's (1980) Defining Issues Test (DIT), an
objective measure of moral judgment based on Kohlberg's
theory, has usually yielded significant positive correlations
with measures of cognitive development, but nonsignificant
correlations with affective and personality measures.
Loevinger and Knoll (1983) and Rest (1980) have identified
the difficulty in administering and scoring Kohlberg's
Moral Judgment Instrument, and Kohlberg has frequently
revised his stages, adding and deleting transitions and sub-
stages (Loevinger & Knoll, 1983). Finally, Sebes and Ford
(1984) have suggested moral development needs to be studied
within the context of broader theoretical frameworks,

investigating "its relationship to affective, interpersonal, cognitive, and psychosocial development" (p. 380).

Few studies have investigated counselors' moral judgment, focusing instead on issues related to counseling ethics (Zahner & McDavis, 1980). Several writers have used Kohlberg's theory as a basis for a model of ethical decision-making in counseling (Van Hoose & Paradise, 1979) and for ethics education (Welfel & Lipsitz, 1983b). In a review of ethics research, Welfel and Lipsitz (1983b) concluded there are no data yet to support the efficacy of ethics education on counselors' actual behavior with clients. They cited the weaknesses of measures of ethical orientation and suggested future studies of ethics should be based in cognitive developmental theories and should include counselor personality variables.

In a comparison of both professional and paraprofessional counselors at various levels of training, Zahner and McDavis (1980) found the professionals had significantly higher levels of moral development than the paraprofessionals as measured by Rest's DIT. Counselors' level of training revealed no differences in moral development scores for either group.

Welfel and Lipsitz (1983a) investigated the relationship of stage of ethical orientation and stage of moral reasoning of counseling students with different levels of experience. Undergraduate seniors majoring in human

development, and beginning, advanced, and doctoral counseling students completed the DIT and the Ethical Judgment
Scale, a new instrument also based on Kohlberg's theory.
Doctoral students scored significantly higher in ethical
orientation than did less experienced students (comparisons
of DIT scores were not reported), and contributions to
professional and social action organizations significantly
correlated with ethical orientation. In addition, stage of
moral reasoning and stage of ethical orientation showed a
significant correlation, although the researchers noted the
weaknesses of the Ethical Judgment Scale and the need for
further validity studies.

Harvey, Hunt, and Schroder

Harvey, Hunt, and Schroder's (1961) conceptual systems
theory specifies four systems or stages to describe a person's style of information processing and ability to adapt
to a changing environment. Stages include cognitive variables (i.e., complexity, integration) and interpersonal
variables or interpersonal orientation (i.e., dependence-
independence, empathy). Higher conceptual systems are
characterized by greater flexibility, complexity, abstract-
ness, interpersonal maturity, self-understanding, and
empathic awareness (Hunt, 1971). The conceptual model has
substantial empirical support, including one study which
found significant correlations between conceptual system and
both moral judgment and ego development (Hunt, 1971; Hunt

& Sullivan, 1974). Two studies of deliberate psychological education included measures of ego development, moral thinking, and conceptual systems also. Teachers and counselors showed significant gains in cognitive complexity in one study (Oja & Sprinthall, 1978), but no signficant increases in the second (Bernier, 1980).

The original conceptual systems theory has been revised separately by the theorists several times. Hunt, for example, now refers to both four stages and three (ABC) stages (Hunt & Sullivan, 1974), and he has focused on elaborating a matching-model of conceptual system and instructional method for more effective education rather than on the developmental model itself. At least four different measures of conceptual systems are reported in the literature (i.e., Conceptual Systems Test, Sentence Completion Test, This I Believe Test, Paragraph Completion Test). These measures assess a person's values and beliefs as a basis for classification into a conceptual system. While the conceptual systems theory describes relevant developmental changes for counselors, the current variations in the stage sequences and in the assessment instruments are confusing for a researcher.

A fairly substantial body of literature has included a measure of conceptual system as a variable in studies of persons in various helping professions, including teachers and counselors, and in studies of counseling-related behaviors. One study indicated that counselors' conceptual

levels are related to their learning styles. Rosenthal
(1977) reported a self-instruction approach for teaching
confrontation skills was more effective with high conceptual level counseling students while guided instruction was
more effective for low level students. These results
reflect the assumptions of Hunt's matching-model for education and parallel results of numerous studies with non-
counseling students (Hunt, 1971; Hunt & Sullivan, 1974).

In related literature, researchers have reported a
relationship between conceptual system and teaching style.
Hunt and Joyce (1967) found a significant correlation
between teachers' conceptual system and their tendency to
use a reflective teaching style, one which encouraged
students to formulate their own theories and to express
themselves. Murphy and Brown (1970) found distinctive
teaching styles for student teachers at each of four conceptual systems. More concrete and dependent student
teachers evidenced a lecturing style, while more abstract
and interdependent student teachers evidenced more
spontaneity in using pupil questions and ideas. They also
encouraged further pupil exploration and led discussions
toward generalizations in a sequential process. Bernier
(1980), in a brief summary of studies of conceptual level
of teachers, found that more complex teachers were more
flexible both cognitively and behaviorally and able to
respond to a wider range of pupils' feelings and experiences. He also concluded that their pupils exhibited higher
cognitive levels and more cooperation and self-exploration.

Several researchers have investigated the relationship between conceptual system and empathy skills. Lutwak and Hennessy (1982), for example, rated tapes of actual counseling interviews conducted by advanced undergraduates and graduates in their first interview skills course. They found highly significant differences between high and low conceptual level students on ratings of accurate empathy. The researchers suggested low level students may be responding from a narrow and dogmatic framework which may affect the counselor-client relationship and alter the direction of counseling.

Other researchers have found a more complex relationship between conceptual system and empathy, reporting significant interactions between conceptual level and other variables. In Heck and Davis's (1973) analogue study, for example, 40 counseling students' written responses to 12 client statements were rated on an accurate empathy scale. High conceptual level students' responses were consistently rated higher, but there was a significant interaction effect between client analogues and students, so that students' empathy levels were not constant across client statements.

Kimberlin and Friesen (1977) gave brief (2 sessions) empathy training to undergraduate students who then wrote responses to videotaped client statements which were designed to be either ambivalent or nonambivalent. Higher conceptual level students wrote more empathic responses to

ambivalent client statements, but there were no significant
differences between high and low level students' responses
to nonambivalent statements. In addition, high level
students wrote significantly more responses which actually
addressed the ambivalence, identifying it or reflecting
both sides of the conflicting emotions. The researchers
concluded the low level students were only able to empathize
with clear-cut emotions, limited in their ability to process
complex, conflicting information. In a similar later study
(Kimberlin & Friesen, 1980), the researchers found the same
differences for both male and female students.

Blaas and Heck (1978) compared students categorized as
having high or low levels of cognitive complexity on five
instruments, including a conceptual systems measure. First
semester counseling students' interactions with two simu-
lated clients were rated on several process variables, including empathic responses. The researchers found no significant differences between high and low complex students
on any of the process variables but did report a significant interaction between empathy ratings and counseling
task (i.e., client) for the low complex students. They
interpreted students' performance on the process variables
other than empathy as more a function of client differences
than their cognitive complexity level. The researchers
concluded cognitive complexity might not be "universally
influential" but affected by situational and environmental
variables.

Strohmer, Biggs, Haase, and Purcell (1983) investigated the effects of level of cognitive complexity and anxiety on first practicum counselors' empathic responses to disabled and nondisabled videotaped clients portrayed by actors. While students with higher complexity scores had higher empathy ratings, the study also found a significant inter- action between disability condition, cognitive complexity, and anxiety. The researchers found that the more complex students showed greater tolerance of anxiety-arousing stimuli and, even more, were able to use the additional stimuli in the disabled client situation to respond more empathically than the less complex students. They described a curvi- linear relationship between cognitive complexity and empathy ratings, with low complex students rated most empathic in situations with minimal levels of arousing stimuli (i.e., nondisabled client and low anxiety), high complex students rated most empathic in situations with moderate levels of arousing stimuli (i.e., either a disabled client or high anxiety), and both groups rated least empathic in situations with maximum arousing stimuli (i.e., disabled client and high anxiety). The researchers suggested the relationship between cognitive complexity and empathy was more complex than previously considered.

Other studies using a measure of conceptual system have investigated the cognitive processing of counselors. Lichtenberg and Heck (1979) analyzed the interactional structure of counselors' and clients' verbal responses in tapes of actual counseling interviews. Students were classified by a total of five measures of cognitive complexity, including a conceptual system measure. More complex students evidenced a somewhat greater degree of variation in their responses than did less complex students, suggesting different information processing styles for high and low conceptual level students. Holloway (1979) reported counselors' conceptual level was moderately related to their formation of clinical hypotheses for videotaped clients.

Goldberg's (1974) analogue study rated beginning counseling students' responses on dimensions reflecting the core conditions (i.e., affective-cognitive, understanding-nonunderstanding, specific-nonspecific, exploratory-nonexploratory) and analyzed them for their interaction style. Students at lower conceptual levels used more direct verbal behavior (e.g., asked questions, gave information or directions), while high level students accepted and used clients' ideas. The most frequent response of all students was asking questions, but low level students' questions asked for information or data, while high level students' questions were more open-ended, encouraging client exploration of beliefs and feelings and client self-responsibility for their replies. In addition, high level or more abstract students were more likely to respond to client affect, to convey an understanding of the client's perspective, and to deal with core rather than peripheral issues. The researchers concluded low level students'

responses reflected actions designed to maintain control of
the interaction.

Finally, Gore (1978) found no relationship between 50
first practicum counselors' conceptual level and their
supervisors' ratings of their effectiveness on the
Counselor Evaluation Rating Scale (CERS).

Kelly

Kelly's (1955) personal construct theory describes a
person's attempts "to discern order in the physical and
interpersonal realities they confront" (Neimeyer & Neimeyer,
1981, p. 190). Persons elaborate their construct systems
to various degrees over time, developing new constructs or
modifying existing ones in an attempt to more accurately
interpret and predict events. This process of elaboration
reflects a developmental pattern, moving toward increasing
levels of complexity and integration in perceptions of self,
others, and life events. The Repertory Grid Technique
(Rep Grid) (Fransella & Bannister, 1977) for studying
constructs yields measures of both cognitive complexity
and integration, and research studies comparing persons
with more and less complexity and integration reflect
developmental differences (Fransella & Bannister, 1977).
Kelly's theory, however, does not specify a developmental
sequence of stages or levels, focusing instead on the
processes of the evolution of the construct systems.

Research using variations of the Rep Grid (Fransella
& Bannister, 1977), one of the measures to be used in this
study, has also studied the relationship of cognitive complexity to the work of persons in the helping professions.
Some studies have compared the behaviors of more and less
complex persons or analyzed the content of their constructs.
Others have identified a developmental pattern in the
changes of their constructs over time which reflect changes
assumed in both the theory of ego development and models of
counselor development.

Two studies have investigated processing of information
about clients. Philip and McCulloch (1968) reported a case
study of a male psychiatric worker who was given the names
of 50 of his former hospitalized patients (role titles or
elements) to use as the basis for eliciting constructs in
two Rep Grids. A cluster analysis identified two main
types of constructs: the impact of the patient on the
psychiatric social worker (i.e., feelings about the patient)
and case conceptualization (i.e., the assessment of social
functioning).

Duehn and Proctor (1974) studied the relationship of
cognitive complexity to social work students' decision-
making processes about clients. While all students used
more pieces of information about clients presented as
similar to themselves than about clients presented as dissimilar, less complex students used significantly fewer
pieces of information with dissimilar clients than did more

complex students. The more complex students also specified
a greater number of alternative interventions, regardless
of the degree of similarity of clients.

Other studies using a Rep Grid have addressed issues
relevant to professional identity and professional development during training. Two relevant studies found a curvilinear relationship between cognitive complexity and amount
of training for teachers (Runkel & Damrin, 1961) and social
work students (Ryle & Breen, 1974). Training or an increase
in knowledge seemed to restrict at first but then enlarge
the subjects' cognitive systems. The untrained subjects
used a large number of dimensions to describe students'
problems (Runkel & Damrin, 1961) and their relationships
with social work clients, supervisors, parents, and self
(Ryle & Breen, 1974), but seemed to use them erratically,
responding to the situation rather than on the basis of
specialized differentiations. Teachers and social work
students with partial training seemed to oversimplify their
construct systems, perhaps attempting to apply a few newly-
learned specific dimensions to all students or relationships. Those with high levels of training seemed to use
their higher number of relevant dimensions to make more
discriminating and specialized perceptions. In addition,
the three Rep Grids completed by the social work students
over the course of their training showed a steady decrease
in the tendency to make polar judgments (extreme ratings)
on the constructs. The social work students thus seemed

to move toward both greater complexity and less dichotomous thinking.

Ben-Peretz and Katz (1983) found significant differences between 145 first and third year female student teachers' constructs describing curriculum materials. While first year student teachers viewed curriculum materials in terms of their more superficial aspects (e.g., "lack of illustration"), third year student teachers looked for the more sophisticated educational aspects and potentials of the curriculum materials (e.g., methods of teaching, level of cognitive domain). The researchers explained the results in terms of a developmental process from relative simplicity to more divergent and professionally-oriented complexity. They concluded experience in the teacher education program helped students develop toward higher levels of professional complexity, rebuilding relevant personal constructs which would guide their educational decisions and actions.

Lifshitz (1974) analyzed the content of the constructs of social workers using standard role titles for 12 representative people to compare the constructs of good social work students and their more experienced supervisors. He found the students used more concrete descriptions (e.g., age, sex, profession) while their supervisors used more abstract descriptions (e.g., diligent, responsible), more intrapsychic and more interpersonal characteristics. In addition, students identified their father, mate, or friend as their professional models, but the supervisors' preferred

models were self, mate, or another social worker with high
ethical standards. In addition, the good social work
students tended to devalue needy people. Lifshitz interpreted these differences as support for a developmental
pattern as students gained experience, characterized by
increasing levels of abstraction and symbolization, inter-
nalization of values, seeing self as a model, and aspiration
toward professional goals.

While these studies illustrate the impact of cognitive
dimensions on teachers' and social workers' perceptions,
thought processes, and changes during training, no relevant
published studies using a Rep Grid have used counselors as
subjects.

Conclusion

The descriptions and/or critiques of these related
theories point to the rationale for choosing Loevinger's
theory of ego development as a basis for this study. Most
obviously, Loevinger has integrated each into her theory
(Loevinger, 1976; Swenson, 1980a). She refers to other
models as separate aspects of the unified ego development
concept, the "central core of personality" (Loevinger &
Knoll, 1983, p. 205). Ego levels describe both cognitive
and interpersonal orientations, both crucial components of
counselor performance. The theory and the instrument
designed to assess the developmental levels has substantial
reliability and validity support (Hauser, 1976; Loevinger,

1979), and recent revisions of each have been refinements
rather than major changes. The Sentence Completion Test's
two-volume manual (Loevinger & Wessler, 1970; Loevinger,
Wessler, & Redmore, 1970) includes comprehensive, detailed
descriptions and examples of responses for each ego level
to aid in scoring. Sentence stems tap a variety of a person's perceptions of experiences and relationships, as opposed to a focus on ethical and moral decisions (i.e.,
Perry and Kohlberg), values and beliefs (i.e., Harvey, Hunt,
& Schroder), or descriptions of self, others, and life
events (i.e., Kelly). For these reasons, ego development
has been chosen as the theoretical basis for this study of
counselor performance and development.

The reviewed research using these developmental theories
or measures based on them illustrate their relevance to
counselor development and supervision education. Since
the theory of ego development encompasses these theories,
the research suggests ego development may be useful in an
exploratory and descriptive study of counselor development.

Summary

Developmental models of supervision education indicate
a pattern of increasing cognitive complexity which impacts
a counselor's perceptions of their clients and behavior
with their clients. The developmental view theorizes these
changes are a result of both experience and individual
differences in the counselors themselves. Research of

developmental models and of individual counselor variables support this view of counselor development, but developmental models have not yet identified and described the possible interaction of individual differences and experience during counselor development.

This study explored the efficacy of the theory of ego development, a comprehensive and established personality stage theory, to describe the differences in counseling students' perceptions of clients, their behavior with clients, and their effectiveness with clients.

CHAPTER III
METHODS AND PROCEDURES

The purpose of the proposed study was to investigate
the efficacy of the theory of ego development as a theoretical basis for counselor development. Counseling students' level of ego development was the independent variable. Because of the exploratory and descriptive nature of
the study, multiple dependent measures of students' counseling performance were used. Students' perceptions of
their clients were assessed by measuring the cognitive
complexity, cognitive integration, and meaningfulness of
their perceptions. In addition, the content of students'
perceptions of their clients were categorized. Other
dependent measures assessed students' behaviors with their
clients, and individual supervisors' ratings of students'
effectiveness with their clients.

Students' age and level of experience (first or second
practica or internship level) were potential confounding
variables. Age has been positively correlated with level
of ego development (Hauser, 1976; Loevinger, 1979;
Loevinger & Wessler, 1970). Level of experience has differentiated between counselors' preferred supervision style
(Moskowitz, 1981; Nash, 1975; Worthington & Roehlke, 1979),
perceptions of their supervisors (Cross & Brown, 1983),

74

relationships with their supervisors (Hill et al , 1981),
and their verbal responses to clients (Cicchetti & Ornston,
1976; Hill et al., 1981). Because of these reported relationships, students' age and level of experience were included in the statistical analysis procedures in this
study.

Subjects

The subjects for this study were University of Florida
counselor education graduate students enrolled in their
first or second counseling practica or internship during
Spring Semester 1984, who were seeing individual clients
and who volunteered to participate. The individual supervisors of the volunteer students were also asked to
participate in the study.

Students

The counselor education program at the University of
Florida is fully accredidated by CACREP and NCATE. All
students are required to complete at least one counseling
practicum, regardless of their chosen program area or
track, in addition to a second practicum and internship in
settings appropriate to their chosen track. To enroll in
their first practica, all students except those in the
counseling psychology track must successfully complete
one-semester courses in Theories of Counseling and Principles of the Counseling Relationship. These students are

76

placed in sites following an interview and selection process
with the hosts at their preferred sites. Requirements for
completing first practica include seeing a minimum of three
clients and reviewing at least 11 tapes with an individual
supervisor, while requirements for second counseling practica and counseling internships vary but are comparable.

To enroll in their first practica, counseling psychology
students must complete two semesters of theoretical counseling
classes. They may also elect to take the Principles of the
Counseling Relationship course. Tapes are not required for
all of their practica and internships.

All practica and internship students meet with their
individual supervisors for one hour per week and, in addition, receive group supervision for one-and-one-half hours
per week either with a faculty member, supervised doctoral
student, or an approved on-site supervisor. University
supervisors contact on-site hosts several times during
the semester. Students are evaluated by their respective
supervisors and hosts at the end of the semester.

Of the 66 graduate students who met the criteria for
participation in the study, a total of 63 volunteered for
one or more parts of the study. Of these 63, 45 were
female and 18 were male, a ratio representative of the
counselor education department's enrollment. The students
represented each program area offered by the department:
school counseling (12), agency counseling (21), counselor
education (4), school psychology (6), student personnel in

higher education (7), and counseling psychology (13).
Twenty students were pursuing a Ph.D. degree; 43, an Ed.S.
degree. The students' ages ranged from 21 to 51 (mean
age=29.95, SD=7.09).

During the time of the study, 27 of the students were
enrolled in their first practicum experience, 10 in their
second practicum, and 26 in their internship experience.
The practica or internship settings represented each student's program area and included public schools, mental
health agencies, the University student counseling centers,
the University residence halls, the University student
services offices, career counseling centers, specialized
service centers (planned parenthood, crisis and suicide
prevention), centers for special populations (rape victims,
juvenile offenders, alcoholics), and support services for
hospitalized patients.

Individual Supervisors

A total of 32 individual supervisors volunteered to
participate in the study, providing ratings for 57 students.
Of these supervisors, 12 were counselor education faculty,
4 were adjunct faculty, 10 were on-site supervisors, and 5
were counselor education and counseling psychology doctoral
students. On-site supervisors had previously been approved by the counselor education department, and doctoral
student supervisors were being supervised by senior
faculty.

One supervisor rated seven students; one rated six
students; two rated four students each, one rated three
students; six rated two students each; and twenty-one
rated one student each.

Instruments

Four instruments were used in this study: the Sentence
Completion Test of Ego Development (Loevinger & Wessler,
1970; Loevinger, Wessler, & Redmore, 1970), the Repertory
Grid Technique (Fransella & Bannister, 1977), the Vanderbilt
Psychotherapy Process Scale (Strupp, 1981), and the Coun-
selor Evaluation Rating Scale (Myrick & Kelly, 1971).

Sentence Completion Test of Ego Development

The independent variable in this study, level of ego
development, was assessed by the Sentence Completion Test
of Ego Development (SCT) (Loevinger & Wessler, 1970;
Loevinger, Wessler, & Redmore, 1970). The SCT is a pro-
jective measure made up of 36 sentence stems (e.g., Raising
a family . . ., When people are helpless . . ., When I am
criticized . . ., When they talked about sex I . . ., Being
with other people . . ., A man's job . . .), with comparable
forms for boys and girls and for men and women. Subjects
are asked to complete each sentence stem in any way they
wish, choosing anyone for references to persons in the
sentence stems.

Scoring procedures

The scoring procedure for the SCT assumes there is a core level of functioning which can be derived from totaling the ratings for each sentence stem (Hauser, 1976; Loevinger & Wessler, 1970). Responses for each item are removed from individual protocols and pooled for rating stem-by-stem rather than by individual total protocol. Each response is rated independently by two trained raters using the item-by-item scoring manual (Loevinger, Wessler, & Redmore, 1970) which contains both categories of responses and illustrative responses for each ego level. Individual protocols are then reassembled and a cumulative frequency distribution of the item scores (ego levels) is tabulated. Total protocol ratings (TPR) are determined by comparing the cumulative frequency distribution to the "automatic ogive rules" (for relatively new raters) or "borderline rules" (for more experienced raters) in the manual (Loevinger & Wessler, 1970). The rules specify the overall ego level of individual protocols. For example, a total protocol rating of I-4 (Conscientious) is given if there are no more than 24 (cumulative total) I-3/4 (Self-aware) items ratings. The cumulative frequency distribution can also be converted to continuous scores by multiplying the number of scores for each ego level by assigned numerical values (1-10 for levels I-2 through I-6) and then adding them for an item sum rating. This continuous score has the advantage of enabling researchers to use regression analyses (e.g., Cox,

1974; Hoppe & Loevinger, 1977), although it has a disadvantage of being more highly correlated with verbal fluency than the TPR ratings based on the ogive rules (Hauser, 1976; Loevinger & Wessler, 1970). Ranges of continuous scores for each ego level have been specified by several researchers (e.g., Hoppe & Loevinger, 1977, Schenberg, cited in Hoppe & Loevinger, 1977).

The SCT manual was developed using samples of female populations ranging in age from 11 to 50+, both black and white, of all marital statuses, who had grade school through graduate college level education. They were employed in a variety of settings or were volunteer workers, and included some psychiatric patients. One group of 22 graduate students in counseling were included in the samples for the evaluation of the manual. Subsequent revisions of the SCT and supplements to the manual have used an even wider data base, including males from backgrounds comparable to and as varied as the original female populations.

The scoring manuals for the SCT include a set of comprehensive and detailed self-trained graduated exercises for new raters. Practice responses for each of the 36 items and complete protocols are followed by answer keys with explanatory notes. Reliability coefficients between personally trained and self-trained raters range from .76 to .92 in a variety of studies, indicating that self-trained raters can achieve the same degree of reliability and produce comparable overall ratings as raters involved in the construction of the manual (Hauser, 1976, Loevinger, 1979; Loevinger & Wessler, 1970).

Reliability and validity

Hauser (1976) reviewed initial reliability studies and although he found some influence of situational factors on subjects' scores, he concluded there was acceptable evidence for test-retest, split-half, and internal consistency reliabilities for the SCT. Loevinger (1979) later reported internal consistency coefficients of about .85 in additional studies. Loevinger and Wessler's (1970) original validity studies found a relationship between SCT scores and age (.74 for boys, .69 for girls), with expected progressive age increases for all ego levels. Hauser's review (1976) pointed to similar age trends.

Loevinger and Wessler (1970) found no significant correlations between SCT scores and verbal fluency or intelligence. Hauser (1976) also concluded the SCT was not simply measuring these factors, although he suggested the relationship of IQ and ego level needed further clarification. Loevinger (1979) found extreme variability in the relation between ego level and IQ, even for similar samples, in later studies.

Hauser (1976) also found tentative evidence for structural validity of the SCT, both for the single factor nature of the theory ("master trait") and for the organization of

psychological variables at specific stages. Loevinger
(1979) discussed evidence for the construct validity of the
SCT in a comprehensive review, including some unpublished
studies. She found general but not decisive support for
theoretical sequentiality, the developmental process of
the stages, in cross-sectional and longitudinal studies.
There were substantial correlations between the SCT and
external criteria such as other developmental stage tests
(e.g., Kohlberg's moral maturity) and behavioral measures
(e.g., conformity, delinquent and helping behaviors).
Correlations with isolated traits specific to stages ranged
widely.

Evidence of validity for low ego levels is primarily
behavioral (e.g., delinquent and deviant behaviors) while
evidence for high ego levels is based in correlations with
attitudes, philosophy of life, self-insight, and ability to
communicate empathy (Loevinger, 1979). Loevinger (1979)
found there was generally positive support for external
validity, although she added that ego development theory
does not clearly define what are positive results. She
concluded the SCT had adequate validity for research purposes if administered and scored properly (i.e., not mailed
to subjects, scored by two trained raters). When used
clinically, she cautioned it should be used in conjunction
with other diagnostic data.

Administration and scoring

Loevinger's instructions for administering and scoring
the SCT were followed in this study (Loevinger & Wessler,
1970; Loevinger, Wessler, & Redmore, 1970). Subjects were
given the SCT in small group settings supervised by an
experienced administrator and trained scorer. The most
recently revised SCT, Form 81, was used. Responses to
individual items on the individual protocols were typed on
separate sheets in random order to insure anonymity. All
responses were scored item-by-item following the scoring
manual by two of three experienced raters (two doctoral
candidates in clinical psychology, one doctoral candidate
in counselor education); one rater scored all the responses.
The raters had 79% perfect agreement on the item responses,
and 93% agreement within a half-step for item responses.
These percentages were quite comparable to those reported
by other investigators (i.e., Hoppe & Loevinger, 1977;
Nettles & Loevinger, 1983). When there was disagreement,
a final rating for each item was determined by consensus or
by a third rater.

Individual protocols were scored using the "automatic
rules" for assigning overall ego levels (TPR ratings). An
item sum score was also tabulated for each protocol, using
the final item ratings, by giving each item score
numerical values as follows: I-2=1, ?/Δ=2, Δ=3, Δ/3=4,
I-3=5, I-3/4=6, I-4=7, I-4/5=8, I-5=9, I-6=10.

Repertory Grid Technique

The students' cognitive perceptions of their clients
were measured by the Repertory Grid Technique (Rep Grid)
(Fransella & Bannister, 1977). The Rep Grid is a technique
based in Kelly's (1955) theory of personal constructs and
his Role Construct Repertory Test. Kelly proposed that
each person continually evolves a unique system of cognitive dimensions or "personal constructs" for interpreting
and predicting events and behavior. This hierarchially
organized system of bipolar personal constructs represents
the individual's attempts to find order and meaning in his/
her experience in the world. The constructs are the abstract verbal labels the individual gives to recurring
themes or the generalizations he/she construes from events
(Neimeyer & Neimeyer, 1981).

The grid technique provides a method to elicit from an
individual a representative sample of the unique personal
constructs he/she uses to interpret and predict behavior
(Fransella & Bannister, 1977; Neimeyer & Neimeyer, 1981).
Typically, subjects are given a standard list of "role
titles" (e.g., your mother, a person with whom you usually
feel most uncomfortable, the happiest person you know
personally) and asked to name the person they know who best
fits that description. This list of "representative
people," called "elements," are presented to the subjects
in triads for comparison. For each triad the subject is

asked to describe a way in which two of them are alike while different from the third. These elicited constructs are the descriptions which comprise the unique personal construct system the subject uses with the particular group of elements elicited by the role titles. The Rep Grid thus provides a vehicle for looking at a person's subjective world (Neimeyer & Neimeyer, 1981), his/her unique interpretations of life experiences, the concepts used to predict events and behaviors of self and others.

The grid technique evolved from Kelly's work in psychotherapy, and so emphasized interpersonal relationships (Fransella & Bannister, 1977). Much research has explored the impact of therapists' and clients' personal construct systems on therapy outcomes (Carr, 1980, Landfield, 1971; Neimeyer & Neimeyer, 1981). The grid technique has been applied, however, to a wide variety of areas, including education, child development, social work, linguistics, politics, social anthropology and urban planning (Fransella & Bannister, 1977; Neimeyer & Neimeyer, 1981). These studies have varied the elements used (e.g., people, maps) in the grid to fit the context of the investigation.

Reliability and validity

Fransella and Bannister (1977) have outlined the problems of establishing traditional measures of reliability and validity for the Rep Grid. Some of these problems stem from the fact that the Rep Grid is a technique rather than a rigid, standardized test. Other problems stem from its basis in personal construct theory itself, which does not assume stability for all types of constructs, for all populations, or for all elements. In addition, since the Rep Grid does not have a specific content (i.e., one set of "items"), validity must be considered in the context of the particular form being used. A variety of grid formats have been used (e.g., rank order, rating grid, implications grid) in different grid matrix sizes (5X5 to 45X45), and they have been analyzed with diverse statistical procedures (e.g., forms of cluster analysis, direct measurement of matching between particular constructs, overall measures of structure) (Fransella & Bannister, 1977; Neimeyer & Neimeyer, 1981).

Various tests of reliability have yielded test-retest coefficients in the range of .30 to .98, including both individuals and groups, for a variety of measures of constructs (e.g., mal-distribution, intensity, factorial similarity) (Fransella & Bannister, 1977). Certain kinds of constructs seem to be used more consistently than others, and different populations vary widely in the stability of constructs in repeat Rep Grids. For example, one study found test-retest coefficients of .6 to .8 for normal and psychiatric populations but a coefficient of .2 for thought disordered populations (Fransella & Bannister, 1977).

In terms of validity, the Rep Grid has discriminated between clinically diagnosed groups, pre- and posttreatment groups, and between normal and psychiatric groups (Fransella & Bannister, 1977) Research has also supported the theoretical description of changes a person makes in his/her construct system in reaction to repeated invalidation or validation of the constructs (Fransella & Bannister, 1977).

Administration and scoring

For the purposes of this study, students were asked to name clients as elements in the grid. Comparison of these elements thus provided a sample of constructs the students used to interpret and predict the behavior of their clients. Students were asked to name actual clients since past studies have indicated a person regards his/her own constructs as more important, meaningful, and useful for describing themselves and others than constructs provided by the experimenters (Adams-Webber, Schwenker, & Barbeau, 1972; Fransella & Bannister, 1977; Landfield, 1971).

To ensure a representative sample of clients, the role titles for naming clients were based on the list suggested by Kelly (in Fransella & Bannister, 1977). This list was reviewed by two Ph.D. psychologists who have conducted extensive research with the Rep Grid, and who have both teaching and therapy experience with personal construct theory. From a list of 21 possible role titles, each reviewer selected the 12 he considered the most representative of Kelly's list and which had the least overlap. The final list of eight role titles was selected to provide a balance of "positive" (e.g., The client who is/was your greatest success) and "negative" (e.g., The client who is/was the hardest for you to understand) role titles for clients. Each of the eight was selected by at least one of the reviewers.

Rating Grid. The rating grid format (described below) was used since it allows greater flexibility of response (Fransella & Bannister, 1977) and analysis of both construct content and structural interrelationships between constructs (Neimeyer & Neimeyer, 1981).

In a semistructured group interview format, students were asked to name the eight clients (elements) who fit each of the descriptions (role titles). They then compared a series of eight triads of these clients. These eight triads were presented in the same sequence for each subject. Following the presentation of each triad, subjects were asked to 1) identify a construct which described how two in the triad are similar, 2) specify the opposite of each elicited construct, providing the polar dimension, and 3) denote their preference between each pair of constructs, giving a positive sign (+) to the preferred construct and a negative sign (-) to the other construct (e.g., + willing to be vulnerable, - keeps distance from feelings; + straightforward, - manipulative).

The students then used the constructs to describe the clients previously named. They rated each of their clients on a Likert-type scale ranging from +3 (the preferred,

positive pole construct strongly describes the client) to
-3 (the negative pole construct strongly describes the
client). A zero rating was used to indicate either that the
construct did not apply to that client or that the two constructs were equally descriptive of the client (Appendix A).

The Rep Grids were analyzed by the FLTORP II computer
program developed by Landfield, Page, and Lavelle. This
analysis provides three relevant continuous scores for an
individual's construct system specific to the role titles
used:

1. <u>Cognitive differentiation/complexity</u>. The Functionally Independent Construction (FIC) score (Landfield,
1971) indicates the number of functionally independent or
separate construct clusters used by the subject. Clusters
are determined by patterns of interrelationships in the
ratings for both persons (elements) and constructs. The
total FIC score is the sum of clusters of functionally
equivalent constructs and clusters of functionally equivalent
persons (Landfield, 1977). Functionally equivalent clusters
indicate those constructs which are dependent on each other;
the subject does not differentiate between these constructs
when rating clients, but instead rates clients similarly on
these constructs. A high FIC score indicates the subject
is using the constructs independently, or is differentiating
between them when rating clients (Neimeyer & Neimeyer,
1981). Low FIC scores indicate a low degree of cognitive

complexity, while a high FIC score indicates a high degree of cognitive complexity.

2. <u>Cognitive integration/Ordination</u>. The Ordination (ORD) score is based on the hierarchial arrangement or organization of the construct system assumed by personal construct theory (Fransella & Bannister, 1977; Neimeyer & Neimeyer, 1981). Using the absolute values of the nonzero ratings, both the number of ratings used and the range of ratings used are computed. The ORD score is the product of these two indices. The computer analysis provides an ORD score for each construct and client and an overall average ORD score (Landfield, 1977). The average score was used in this study.

The ORD score indicates to what degree of flexibility a subject uses constructs to rate clients (elements) (Fransella & Bannister, 1977; Neimeyer & Neimeyer, 1981). Thus it describes to what degree a subject considers "shades of meaning" between the poles of a construct (Landfield, 1977). The more integrated subject is using a more elaborate construct system, one with integrative, "superordinate" constructions. A low ORD score indicates the subject sees few connections between events, while an extremely high score indicates the subject construes interrelations between almost all events (Landfield, 1977).

3. <u>Meaningfulness/Extremity</u>. The Extremity Score (EXTR) has been used as an indication of the "meaningfulness" of the subject's constructs and elements (Neimeyer &

Neimeyer, 1981), with the more extreme ratings (+3 and -3) reflecting more meaningfulness. The sum of the absolute values of all ratings, the EXTR score indicates how polarized the ratings are (Landfield, 1977). More extreme ratings have been usually found on constructs elicited from subjects than on constructs supplied to subjects (Fransella & Bannister, 1977).

Content analysis. Students' constructs were also subjected to a content analysis. Constructs were classified into one of four content categories established by Duck (1973) during a series of studies investigating the developmental stages of friendship formation. As described by Duck, these content categories represent a continuum of more literal and concrete to more conceptual and abstract constructs. They describe progression up a hierarchy from viewing others "in terms of 'stereotypes' to a greater individuation and differentiation of them" (p. 141) during the formation of personal relationships. His four content categories in progressive order are the following:

1. Physical characteristics or factual information (e.g., tall-short; long hair-short hair; American-Spanish).

2. Interactional style (e.g., talkative-quiet; warm-aloof; gesticulates-restrains gestures).

3. Roles or habitual activities (e.g., parent-child; teacher-student; sings and plays guitar-can't do either).

4. Psychological characteristics, including personality and cognitive attributes (e.g., sensitive-insensitive;

ambitious-not ambitious; interested in people-interested in self).

According to Duck (1973), psychological constructs are more cognitively complex and require a more integrated use of these deeper-level constructs in describing others. He also describes a person who more frequently uses psychological constructs as one who has more potential for developing social skills and abilities.

In Duck's (1973) series of studies, two or three independent raters achieved interrater reliability in the range of .75 to .90. In this study, two trained counselor education graduate students independently rated each construct of all the students. The raters had 78% perfect agreement; on disagreements, consensus was reached for all of the constructs. The total number of constructs classified into each category was used as a categorial variable measure of the content of the students' descriptions (constructs) of their clients (elements).

Appropriateness to the study

The grid technique was developed in the context of Kelly's (1955) personal construct theory. Fransella and Bannister (1977) have cautioned against the use of the technique independent of the theory Loevinger (1976) specified Kelly as one of the theorists she incorporated into ego development theory, and personal construct theory and ego development theory describe similar patterns of

personality development. Therefore it seemed appropriate
to use the Rep Grid in this study. The Rep Grid offered a
means of studying both the structure and content of counselors' specific and unique perceptions of their clients,
and thus was a vehicle for identifying differences in perceptions of counselors at various levels of ego development.

Vanderbilt Psychotherapy Process Scales

The students' behavior with clients was assessed by
the Vanderbilt Psychotherapy Process Scales (VPPS) (O'Malley,
Suh, & Strupp, 1983; Strupp, 1981). The VPPS was developed
during the Vanderbilt Psychotherapy Research Project, a
long range study of time-limited therapy, to assess those
characteristics of the patient and therapist and their
interaction which might relate to therapy outcome. The VPPS
includes both positive and negative aspects of those patient
and therapist behaviors and attitudes the authors assume
either facilitate or impede progress in therapy. Items were
designed to be applicable to a broad range of theoretical
orientations and therapeutic interventions, and to be more
descriptive than evaluative. Published research to date has
been conducted by the Vanderbilt research team and has
primarily investigated the relationship of therapy and outcome (Suh, O'Malley, & Strupp, in press).

As a part of the research project, the VPPS has been
field-tested, statistically analyzed, and refined several
times. The current revised form (Strupp, 1981) consists of

80 Likert-type items scored on an ordinal scale ranging
from 1 (not at all) to 5 (a great deal). The two major
sections of the VPPS include items addressing patient behavior and attitudes and items dealing with therapist behavior and attitudes. In addition, three global ratings
assess the quality of the relationship, the productivity
of the session, and the patient's current level of functioning.

Factor analyses of the items of the current form
(O'Malley et al., 1983) and a similar previous form (Gomes-
Schwartz, 1978) yielded comparable subscales, including
Patient Participation, Patient Hostility, Patient Exploration, Therapist Exploration, Therapist Warmth and Friendliness, and Negative Therapist Attitude. A subscale score is
the sum of the scores for the relevant items; subscale
scores have been used in past research rather than a total
VPPS score. Internal consistency of these subscales in
the revised form range from .82 to .96. A modified 35-
item intake version is also available.

Rating procedures

Multiple raters complete the VPPS after reviewing a
videotape or audiotape of an actual therapy session. Studies
using the VPPS have reported interrater reliability coefficients ranging from .79 to .94. Ratings made from
transcripts have been found generally less reliable than
those made from videotapes or audiotapes, especially for the

subscales Therapist Warmth and Friendliness, Negative Therapist Attitude, and Patient Hostility. In addition, supplementing audiotapes and videotapes with transcripts have not increased the reliability of ratings of the tapes alone (Suh et al., in press).

A recent manual (Strupp, 1981) defines each item and illustrates extreme (1 or 5) and average (3) ratings for most items. Raters are instructed to take the position of a "generalized other," an outside observer of the patient and therapist and their interaction. Objective criteria are emphasized; inferences are discouraged. Raters with little clinical experience have demonstrated reliable ratings by using the scoring manual, indicating only a minimum level of inference is made in ratings (Suh et al., in press). The authors suggest raters should be trained to a criterion level of interrater reliability of .90 (Suh et al., in press).

Based on past studies, 15-minute segments are considered adequate for rating the process characteristics assessed by the VPPS (Suh et al., in press). While both random and systematic sampling of tapes have been used, the systematic sampling procedure (first, middle, and closing 5 minute segments) has the advantage of providing raters with an overview of the entire process of the therapy session (Suh et al., in press). Past research studies have indicated ratings of early therapy sessions are critically important to therapy outcome, in particular, the course of therapy has seemed to be established by the third session (Suh et al., in press).

Administration and rating

Forty-five of the volunteer counseling students each submitted an audiotape of a "working" counseling session (at least third session) with a client. One inaudible tape was dropped from the study, so that a total of 44 audiotapes were rated.

For the purposes of this study, the 44 students' audiotapes were sampled and rated using the systematic sampling procedure and the VPPS items assessing therapist behavior and attitude (items 44-80). These items include three subscales. Therapist Warmth and Friendliness items assess the therapist's display of warmth and emotional involvement with the client (e.g., "Helped the patient feel accepted in the relationship," "Optimistic"). Negative Therapist Attitude items describe attitudes that might intimidate or threaten the client (e.g., "Explicitly tried to impose his or her values on the patient," "Judgmental"). Therapist Exploration items assess attempts to examine the psychodynamics underlying the client's problems (e.g., "Tried to help the patient understand the reasons behind his or her actions," "Identified themes in the patient's behavior and experiences").

The ratings on the 37 therapist behavior and attitude items were summed to form a total score, so that higher

total scores indicated higher ratings of therapist behavior
and attitudes related to positive therapy outcome. This
total score was a continuous variable measure of students'
behavior with clients.

Raters of the audiotapes were an advanced doctoral
counseling student and a Ph.D. counselor. Both had had
experience rating counseling students' tapes using the Gazda
et al. (1977) scale and had supervised practicum students.
The two raters were trained on the item definitions in the
manual using anonymous tapes of actual therapy sessions
which were not a part of the study. Their independent ratings of the tapes used in this study had a 86 interrater
reliability coefficient. This level of reliability falls
within the acceptable range reported by other researchers
(Suh et al., in press).

Counselor Evaluation Rating Scale

The students' effectiveness with their clients was
measured by the Counselor Evaluation Rating Scale (CERS)
(Myrick & Kelly, 1971). The CERS was designed to be used
by a supervisor to evaluate a counselor's performance in
both counseling and supervisory sessions. It consists of
27 Likert-type (-3 to +3) items, 13 comprise the counseling
performance subscale; another 13, the supervision subscale.
For scoring purposes, scaled scores from 1 (-3) to 7 (+3)
are used. The two subscale ratings are summed (after re-
versing ratings on negative items) with the rating on the

final item ("Can be recommended for a counseling position without reservation") for a total rating of counselor effectiveness. The total score range (27-189) provides a wide range for differentiating counselor effectiveness, important for research purposes (Myrick & Kelly, 1971). The CERS has been widely used as an educational and research tool (Hansen, Robins, & Grimes, 1982; Loesch & Rucker, 1977).

The CERS was designed to be a comprehensive evaluation measure of counselor effectiveness. Item content includes not only the facilitative conditions, but also more advanced counselor behaviors (e.g., "Is sensitive to dynamics of self in counseling relationships") and counseling-relevant behaviors primarily exhibited in supervision rather than in counseling sessions (e.g., "Can explain what is involved in counseling and discuss intelligently its objectives").

Reliability and validity

Myrick and Kelly (1971) reported a split-half reliability coefficient of .95, a test-retest reliability coefficient of .94, and a correlation of .86 for the two subscales. Jones (1974) reported split-half reliability at .87 for CERS ratings in his study. Myrick and Kelly (1971) also reported negligible or even negative correlations between counselors' CERS scores and GRE scores (-.03) and between counselors' CERS scores and undergraduate GPA (-.25).

Jones (1974) challenged the validity of the CERS after finding only one positive relationship between the three scale scores of the CERS and Carkhuff's rating scales for empathy, respect, and genuineness for 19 practicum students. Since the CERS was designed as a more comprehensive evaluation measure (Myrick & Kelly, 1971), as Jones noted, the insignificant correlations may be at least in part a result of the fact that the CERS includes behaviors other than the facilitative conditions, and includes both counseling and supervision behaviors.

Loesch and Rucker (1977) conducted a factor analysis of the CERS using ratings of approximately 35 supervisors for 404 students. They found six primary factors (general counseling performance, professional attitude, counseling behavior, counseling knowledge, supervision attitude, and supervision behavior) and two second order factors (counseling and supervision). Since they found the counseling and supervision second-order factors were not completely independent, Loesch and Rucker (1977) suggested the total CERS score might be a more valid score than the two subscale scores. The CERS does not evaluate either highly specific counseling and supervision behaviors, or performance in terms of outcome, they added.

For the purposes of this study, the total CERS score given by the individual supervisor for each student was used, as recommended by Loesch and Rucker (1977), to provide one continuous variable score of overall counselor effectiveness.

Appropriateness to the study

Myrick and Kelly (1971) designed items which tap a counselor's perceptions of clients and the counselor's behavior with clients, the two other dependent variables in this study. The CERS, however, provided a means of assessing these variables in terms of their effectiveness, rather than being primarily descriptive, as were the other measures of these variables. Use of the CERS also provided input from a person who had regularly observed a student over a semester, interacted with a student personally each week, reviewed tapes of a variety of a student's clients, and heard a student's case presentations of clients. The individual supervisor thus had a perspective on the student's progress and development of skills and professional identity which the other dependent measures by design did not provide.

Data Collection

All counselor education students who were enrolled in a first or second counseling practica or internship for Spring Semester 1984 were invited to participate in this study.

Each student received a letter via mail or in person during group supervision meetings during the first three weeks of the semester (Appendix B). Both presentations of the study explained the general nature of the study and what was needed from each participant (i.e., completing two instruments, making an audiotape to be rated, and being rated by the individual supervisor). A release form (Appendix C) to be completed by the client the student would choose for audiotaping was included with the letter. In follow-up phone calls and/or during the group supervision meetings, students were asked to choose one of several small group sessions scheduled during the midweek of the semester for administration of the two assessment instruments. They were also asked to bring to the testing session the counseling audiotape and the signed client release form.

During all contacts with the investigator, the students were encouraged to ask any questions about the study and/or their participation. Confidentiality was stressed, giving the students full assurance that none of the data collected would be seen by any of their supervisors, and that it would have no bearing on their evaluations or grades for their practica or internships.

The test administration for each small group followed the same format. The students were asked to read and sign a release form (Appendix C) and complete a general data sheet (Appendix E). The general nature of the study was explained and any further questions were answered at that time. The release form was marked with an identification number which was the only identification used on the assessment instruments, audiotapes, and supervisors' ratings.

The students' audiotapes of their third counseling session and signed client release forms were numbered and collected. The students were administered the Repertory

Grid Technique first, then asked to complete the Sentence Completion Test. Specific procedures for administering each instrument are included in the individual instrument sections of this chapter.

Letters were mailed early in the semester to all the individual supervisors of the participating students (Appendix F). The letters explained the general nature of the study and asked the supervisor to agree to complete a Counselor Evaluation Rating Scale (CERS) for each supervisee during the tenth week of the semester, a procedure which required about 15 minutes. The letter specified that the CERS and complete instructions would be mailed to them at that time.

During the tenth week of the semester, the individual supervisor of each student participant was mailed a copy of the CERS (one per supervisee), a letter of instructions (Appendix G) for completing the scale, and a stamped return envelope. The letter paired each student with his/her identification number; the CERS was marked only with the student's identification number. The supervisors were asked to return the CERS to the researcher within one week.

Null Hypotheses

The following null hypotheses were tested:

1. There is no significant relationship (.05 setwise criterion level) between the level of cognitive complexity of students' perceptions of their clients and

students' levels of ego development after controlling for students' age and levels of experience.

2. There is no significant relationship (.05 set-wise criterion level) between the level of cognitive integration of students' perceptions of their clients and students' levels of ego development after controlling for students' age and levels of experience.

3. There is no significant relationship (.05 set-wise criterion level) between the level of meaningfulness of students' perceptions of their clients and students' levels of ego development after controlling for students' age and levels of experience.

4. There is no significant relationship (.05 set-wise criterion level) between students' behavior with their clients and students' levels of ego development after controlling for students' age and levels of experience.

5. There is no significant relationship (.05 set-wise criterion level) between supervisors' ratings of students' counseling effectiveness with their clients and students' levels of ego development after controlling for students' age and levels of experience.

6. There is no significant relationship (.05 criterion level) between the content categories of students' perceptions of their clients and students' level of ego development.

Statistical Analysis

A series of five separate multiple regression analyses were conducted to test the first five null hypotheses. Since ego level and age were not significantly correlated for this population ($r=.0825$, $p=.5204$), age was not included in the planned regression equation. Partial correlations controlling for level of experience (LEXP) were computed between ego level (EGO) (item sum scores) and each of the five dependent variables (FIC, ORD, EXTR, CERS, VPPS). Each regression equation had the following form·

$$\hat{Y} = \alpha + \beta_1(EGO) + \beta_2(LEXP) + \varepsilon.$$

A Chi-square test of differences was used to test the sixth hypothesis, computing the total frequency of constructs in each content category across ego levels.

CHAPTER IV
ANALYSIS AND RESULTS

The results of the study are presented in this chapter. In the first section, descriptive data for the independent variable, level of ego development (EGO), and for each of the dependent variables (FIC, ORD, EXTR, VPPS, CDRS, Content Categories) are summarized. Tables 4 and 5 summarize descriptive data for each level of ego development and level of experience represented by the subjects. In the second section of the chapter, the results for each null hypothesis are presented.

Descriptive Data

Level of Ego Development (EGO)

The 63 students in this study represented five levels of ego development: 1 was classified as Delta (Δ), 1 as Conformist (I-3), 16 as Self-aware (I-3/4), 39 as Conscientious (I-4), and 6 as Individualistic (I-4/5). As suggested by Swenson (1980b), most of the graduate students in this study scored at the Conscientious (I-4) level. Item sum scores ranged from 181 to 251 (mean EGO=219.57, SD= 14.48, median=220, mode=216).

TABLE 4

MEANS AND STANDARD DEVIATIONS FOR COUNSELING VARIABLES BY LEVEL OF EGO DEVELOPMENT

Counseling Variable	Level of Ego Development					
	Delta (Δ) n=1	Conformist (I-3) n=1	Self-aware (I-3/4) n=16	Conscientious (I-4) n=39	Individualistic (I-4/5) n=6	Total n=63
AGE						
Mean	36	45	27.69	30.21	30.83	29.95
SD	–	–	6.18	7.47	3.60	7.09
LEXP						
Mean	1	2	1.88	1.97	2.50	1.98
SD	–	–	0.96	0.93	0.84	0.92
FIC						
Mean	6	4	8.56	8.10	6.50	7.97
SD	–	–	3.22	3.27	2.66	3.20
ORD						
Mean	10.5	9.5	9.22	9.46	9.38	9.41
SD	–	–	1.58	1.76	1.74	1.68
EXTR						
Mean	2.05	1.67	2.21	2.02	2.13	2.08
SD	–	–	0.30	0.28	0.26	0.29
VPPS	n=1	n=1	n=13	n=26	n=3	n=44
Mean	197.00	202.00	206.62	214.77	221.67	212.14
SD	–	–	31.10	33.36	25.81	31.23
CERS	n=1	n=1	n=15	n=36	n=1	n=57
Mean	182.00	71.00	171.00	164.61	176.75	165.81
SD	–	–	16.87	21.07	9.46	23.14

Note. LEXP = Level of experience; FIC = Functionally Independent Constructions (cognitive complexity); ORD = Ordination score (cognitive integration); EXTR = Extremity score (meaningfulness of constructs); VPPS = Vanderbilt Psychotherapy Process Scales; CERS = Counselor Evaluation Rating Scale.

TABLE 5

MEANS AND STANDARD DEVIATIONS FOR COUNSELING
VARIABLES BY LEVEL OF EXPERIENCE

Counseling Variable	Level of Experience			
	First Practicum n=27	Second Practicum n=10	Internship n=26	Total n=63
AGE				
Mean	29.78	27.90	30.92	29.95
SD	8.00	6.38	6.37	7.09
EGO				
Mean	217.89	216.00	222.69	219.57
SD	15.04	15.18	13.54	14.48
FIC				
Mean	7.78	7.60	8.31	7.97
SD	3.45	2.72	3.20	3.20
ORD				
Mean	9.35	9.33	9.50	9.41
SD	1.77	1.43	1.72	1.68
EXTR				
Mean	2.11	1.95	2.09	2.08
SD	0.28	0.29	0.29	0.29
VPPS	n=23	n=7	n=14	n=44
Mean	204.65	214.43	223.29	212.14
SD	28.88	16.60	38.10	31.23
CERS	n=27	n=9	n=21	n=57
Mean	164.44	152.44	173.29	165.81
SD	16.03	41.71	18.09	23.14

Note. EGO = Ego level, item sum scores; FIC = Functionally
Independent Constructions (cognitive complexity), ORD =
Ordination score (cognitive integration); EXTR = Extremity
score (meaningfulness of constructs); VPPS = Vanderbilt
Psychotherapy Process Scales; CERS = Counselor Evaluation
Rating Scale.

Structural Cognitive Variables

The 63 students' perceptions of their clients reported
on the Rep Grid were analyzed to determine the degrees of
complexity (FIC), integration (ORD), and meaningfulness
(EXTR) of these cognitions.

The FIC scores, measuring the degree of complexity of
the students' perceptions, ranged from 3 to 15 (mean FIC=
7.97, SD=3.20, median=7, mode=6). Students at the higher
ego level had a lower mean FIC score, while the most experienced students had a higher mean FIC score.

The ORD scores, measuring the degree of integration of
the students' perceptions, ranged from 3.75 to 11.75 (mean
ORD=9.41, SD=1.68, median=9.50, mode=9.50. Mean ORD scores
were fairly stable across ego levels and experience levels.

The EXTR scores, measuring the degree of meaningfulness of the students' perceptions, ranged from 1.34 to 2.60
(mean EXTR=2.08, SD=0.29, median=2.06, mode=2.06). Mean
EXTR scores were fairly stable across ego levels and experience levels.

Students' Counseling Behavior (VPPS)

The audiotapes of counseling sessions submitted by 44
students in this study were rated on the VPPS for the degree
of therapist behavior and attitude related to positive
therapy outcome. The VPPS ratings ranged from 154 to 267
(mean VPPS=212.14, SD=31.23, median=207.50, mode=206).

There was a pattern of increasing mean VPPS scores across both ego levels and experience levels.

Supervisors' Effectiveness Ratings (CERS)

The 57 students who were rated for their overall counseling effectiveness by their individual supervisors on the CERS had scores ranging from 71 to 189 (mean CERS= 165.81, SD=23.14, median=170, mode=189). Four students received perfect scores (189), and 24% had scores of 182 or higher. There was a curvilinear pattern of mean CERS scores across both ego levels and experience levels. Scores at the Conscientious ego level (I-4) were lower than the scores at Self-aware(I-3/4) and Individualistic (I-4/5), and scores at second practicum were lower than those at first practicum and internship.

Content Categories

A total of 504 pairs of constructs were generated by the 63 subjects (8 per subject). Almost three-fourths of the constructs were classified as either psychological (38.49%) or interactional (35.91%). Smaller numbers of constructs were classified as either role (17.06%) or physical (8.53%). Frequency distributions of constructs classified into each category by ego level and by experience level are summarized in Tables 6 and 7.

110

TABLE 6

FREQUENCY OF CONSTRUCTS CLASSIFIED INTO EACH CONTENT CATEGORY
BY LEVEL OF EGO DEVELOPMENT

Ego Level	Content Category				
	Physical	Interactional	Role	Psychological	Total
Delta (Δ)					
Frequency	0	3	2	3	8
Percentage	0.00%	0.60%	0.40%	0.60%	1.59%
Conformist (I-3)					
Frequency	1	3	0	4	8
Percentage	0.20%	0.60%	0.00%	0.79%	1.59%
Self-aware (I-3/4)					
Frequency	18	37	17	56	128
Percentage	3.57%	7.34%	3.37%	11.11%	25.40%
Conscientious (I-4)					
Frequency	22	114	59	117	312
Percentage	4.36%	22.62%	11.70%	23.21%	61.90%
Individualistic (I-4/5)					
Frequency	2	24	8	14	48
Percentage	0.40%	4.76%	1.59%	2.78%	9.52%
Total					
Frequency	43	181	86	194	504
Percentage	8.53%	35.91%	17.06%	38.49%	100.00%

TABLE 7

FREQUENCY OF CONSTRUCTS CLASSIFIED INTO EACH CONTENT CATEGORY BY LEVEL OF EXPERIENCE

Level of Experience	Content Category				
	Physical	Interactional	Role	Psychological	Total
First Practicum					
Frequency	17	87	34	78	216
Percentage	3.37%	17.26%	6.75%	15.48%	42.86%
Second Practicum					
Frequency	4	33	16	27	80
Percentage	0.79%	6.55%	3.17%	5.36%	15.87%
Internship					
Frequency	22	61	36	89	208
Percentage	4.37%	12.10%	7.14%	17.66%	41.27%
Total					
Frequency	43	181	86	194	504
Percentage	8.53%	35.91%	17.07%	38.49%	100.00%

Results of Statistical Analyses

The results of the multiple regression analyses of counselor variables with levels of ego development are displayed in Table 8. To summarize the results, each null hypothesis is presented separately.

Hypothesis 1. There is no signficant relationship (.05 set-wise criterion level) between the level of cognitive complexity of students' perceptions of their clients and students' levels of ego development after controlling for students' levels of experience.

The partial correlation computed between ego level (EGO) and the level of cognitive complexity of students' perceptions of their clients (FIC) controlling for level of experience (LEXP) was not significant, $F(1, 60) = 0.67$, p=.4155. Thus, the first null hypothesis was not rejected.

Hypothesis 2. There is no significant relationship (.05 set-wise criterion level) between the level of cognitive integration of students' perceptions of their clients and students' levels of ego development after controlling for students' levels of experience.

The partial correlation computed between ego level (EGO) and the level of cognitive integration of students' perceptions of their clients (ORD) controlling for level of experience (LEXP) was not significant, $F(1, 60) = 0.08$, p=.7805. Thus, the second null hypothesis was not rejected.

TABLE 8

MULTIPLE REGRESSION ANALYSES OF COUNSELING VARIABLES WITH LEVELS
OF EGO DEVELOPMENT

Dependent Variable	n	Regression Coefficient	Partial r	R^2	F	df	p
FIC	63	-0.0235	-.1053	.0168	0.67	1,60	.4155
ORD	63	0.0423	.0361	.0030	0.08	1,60	.7805
EXTR	63	-0.0002	-.0090	.0011	0.00	1,60	.9464
VPPS	44	0.5453	.2734	.1422	3.31	1,41	.0763
CERS	57	0.3286	.2102	.0693	2.49	1,54	.1206

Note. FIC = Functionally Independent Constructions (cognitive complexity); ORD = Ordination score (cognitive integration), EXTR = Extremity score (meaningfulness of constructs);
VPPS = Vanderbilt Psychotherapy Process Scales; CERS = Counselor Evaluation Scale.
R^2 coefficients are for the regression equation including EGO and LEXP.
F values for all variables are partial F values used to test the significance of the
relationships with level of ego development, level of experience partialed out.
None of the partial F values were significant at the .05 set-wise criterion level.

Hypothesis 3. There is no significant relationship
(.05 set-wise criterion level) between the level of meaningfulness of students' perceptions of their clients and
students' levels of ego development after controlling for
students' levels of experience.

The partial correlation computed between ego level
(EGO) and the level of meaningfulness of students' perceptions of their clients (EXTR) controlling for level of
experience (LEXP) was not significant, $F(1, 60) = 0.00$,
$p=.9464$. Thus, the third null hypothesis was not rejected.

Hypothesis 4. There is no significant relationship
(.05 set-wise criterion level) between students' behavior
with their clients and students' levels of ego development
after controlling for students' levels of experience.

The partial correlation computed between ego level
(EGO) and students' behavior with their clients (VPPS)
controlling for level of experience (LEXP) was not significant, $F(1, 41) = 3.31$, $p=.0763$. Thus, the fourth null
hypothesis was not rejected.

Hypothesis 5. There is no significant relationship
(.05 set-wise criterion level) between supervisors' ratings
of students' counseling effectiveness with their clients
and students' levels of ego development after controlling
for students' levels of experience.

The partial correlation computed between ego level
(EGO) and supervisors' ratings of students' counseling
effectiveness (CERS) controlling for level of experience

(LEXP) was not significant, F(1, 54) = 2 49, p=.1206. Thus, the fifth null hypothesis was not rejected.

Hypothesis 6. There is no significant relationship (.05 criterion level) between the content categories of students' perceptions of their clients and students' levels of ego development.

A 3 (ego level) X 4 (content category) Chi-square test of differences was used to analyze the relationship of students' levels of ego development and the content categories of their constructs describing their perceptions of their clients. For the purposes of the Chi-square test, subjects were grouped into three levels of ego development. The Delta (n=1), Conformist (n=1), and Self-aware (n=16) subjects formed one group; the Conscientious (n=39) subjects and the Individualistic (n=6) subjects formed two separate groups. These groupings were chosen to avoid empty cells for the lowest ego levels and were based on the major theoretical shift from Self-aware to Conscientious. The groupings also allowed for an analysis of the categories used by the higher Individualistic subjects. The content categories were based on Duck's (1973) four-level classification system: physical, interactional, role, psychological.

The Chi-square test of ego levels and content categories is presented in Table 9. The Chi-square test of differences yielded a significant difference between the

TABLE 9

CHI-SQUARE OF CONSTRUCTS CLASSIFIED INTO EACH CONTENT CATEGORY BY
LEVEL OF EGO DEVELOPMENT

Ego Level	Content Category				
	Physical	Interactional	Role	Psychological	Total
Delta (Δ) Conformist (I-3) Self-aware (I-3/4) N=18	19 3.77 13.19 44.19	43 8.53 29.86 23.76	19 3.77 13.19 22.09	63 12.50 43.75 32.47	144 28.57
Conscientious (I-4) N=39	22 4.37 7.05 51.16	111 22.62 36.54 62.98	59 11.71 18.91 68.60	117 23.21 37.50 60.31	312 61.90
Individualistic (I-4/5) N=6	2 0.40 4.17 4.65	24 4.76 50.00 13.26	8 1.59 16.67 9.30	14 2.78 29.17 7.22	48 9.52
Total N=63	43 8.53	181 35.91	86 17.06	194 38.49	504 100.00

Note. The numbers in each cell represent Frequency
Percent
Row percent
Column percent.

$x^2 = 13.788$ df=6   p=.0321

frequency of content categories at the three ego levels, χ^2 (6) = 13.788 (p=.0321), and the sixth null hypothesis was rejected. While the majority of constructs at each ego level were classified as either interactional or psychological, there were changes in the frequencies across ego levels. From lower to higher ego level groups there was a consistent decline in the frequency of physical constructs and psychological constructs, and a consistent increase in interactional constructs. In addition, constructs of pre-Conscientious students were primarily classified as psychological (43.75%); constructs of Conscientious students were more evenly distributed; and half of the constructs of Individualistic students were classified as interactional (50.00%).

Post-hoc Analyses

Results of the planned analyses and the means for the counselor variables suggested several additional statistical tests. These are reported in the following sections.

Structural measures of students' perceptions of clients

None of the cognitive measures of students' client construct systems had a significant linear relationship with the students' levels of ego development. Neither the degree of cognitive complexity, integration, or extremity (meaningfulness) of the perceptions of clients were related to the degree of sophistication of ego development. An

examination of the range of FIC scores and the means of the
FIC and ORD scores suggested an additional analysis which
would consider combinations of students' levels of complexity and integration. As suggested by Landfield (1977),
four combinations of FIC and ORD scores were used to create
four quadrants of high and low scores:

Quadrant 1--Low complexity (FIC), low integration (ORD)

Quadrant 2--Low complexity (FIC), high integration (ORD)

Quadrant 3--High complexity (FIC), low integration (ORD)

Quadrant 4--High complexity (FIC), high integration

(ORD)

Students were placed in one of the quadrants based on
median splits of FIC (low FIC < 7; high FIC > =7) and ORD
(low ORD < 9.5, high ORD > =9.5) scores.

A 2 (FIC) X 2 (ORD) factorial analysis of variance was
computed for the ego level item sum scores (Appendix H).
While the interaction of FIC and ORD was not statistically
significant, $F(1, 59) = 2.60$, p=.1121, the suggested relationship was stronger than the relationships found in the
separate regression analyses for FIC and ORD. Based on
the mean ego level item sum scores for each quadrant,
students in Quadrant 1 (mean EGO=222.92, n=13) and Quadrant
4 (mean EGO=221.36, n=25) tended to have higher ego levels
than did students in Quadrant 2 (mean EGO=214.58, n=12)
and Quadrant 3 (mean EGO=217.38, n=13). Students at higher
levels of ego development tended to use construct systems

to describe their clients which were either low in both complexity and integration or were high in both complexity and integration

Supervisors' effectiveness ratings (CERS)

Individual supervisors' ratings of students' counseling effectiveness (CERS) with their clients did not have a significant linear relationship with the students' levels of ego development in a regression analysis controlling for students' levels of experience. An examination of the CERS means by ego level (EGO) and by level of experience (LEXP) (see Tables 4 and 5) suggested separate post-hoc regressional analyses for each of these variables. The results of these analyses are summarized in Appendices I and J. In a simple regression analysis, there was a suggestion of a positive linear relationship between CERS and EGO, $F(1, 55) = 2.97$, $p=.0907$). There was a significant curvilinear relationship between CERS and LEXP, $F(1, 54) = 4.06$, $p=.0490$), with students in their second practicum receiving the lowest CERS ratings.

CHAPTER V
CONCLUSIONS

The purpose of this study was to explore the relationship of the theory of ego development and counselor development in order to investigate the efficacy of ego development as a theoretical basis for models of counselor development. To more fully study the problem, multiple counseling variables were included· the structure and content of counseling students' perceptions of their clients, counseling students' interactions with their clients, and individual supervisors' ratings of their students' overall counseling effectiveness.

The results of the study provide only partial support for the theoretical hypotheses that 1) counseling students functioning at higher levels of ego development would have more highly developed cognitions about their clients, 2) would have more positive interactions with their clients, and 3) would be rated as more effective by their individual supervisors. While only one of the main tests yielded statistically significant results, near significant results and post-hoc analyses suggested some support for the theoretical assumptions tested and generated additional hypotheses which warrant further study.

These results and conclusions are discussed in this
chapter. The limitations of the study are outlined in the
first section and the results of the statistical analyses
are discussed in the next section. Implications for future
research are then presented, followed by a summary of the
conclusions of the study.

Limitations of the Study

Several limitations of the study may have contributed
to the failure to find significant relationships. These
factors also need to be considered when interpreting the
results of the study.

Because of its exploratory, descriptive nature, this
study exercised limited control over the variables included.
As a result, there were differential numbers of counseling
students at the levels of ego development and levels of
experience. Only five of the ten ego levels were represented, with most students (71%) at or above the Conscientious (I-4) stage, and only one student each at the
Delta (Δ) and Conformist (I-3) stages. The restricted
range of ego levels limited analysis of differences in the
counseling variables between ego levels, although the use
of continuous scores (item sum scores) in some analyses
somewhat compensated for this limitation.

Counseling students were in a wide variety of practica
and internship settings, were seeing clients ranging from
public school students to alcoholic adults, and were dealing

with issues ranging from developmental concerns to suicidal tendencies. Students were thus reporting perceptions of dissimilar client populations on the Rep Grid and responding to diverse counseling concerns on their respective audio-tapes. In addition, 32 individual supervisors rated 57 students' counseling effectiveness. It is unknown how these supervisors differed in their supervision styles, interactions with their students, requirements for the semester, and evaluation procedures. The study also excluded any consideration of the supervisors' ego levels.

It is also unknown in what ways the 19 students who did not contribute an audiotape differed from those who did submit a tape. Policies and/or procedures at several sites prohibited taping for research purposes. Some students, however, opted not to participate in this part of the study. The 19 students who did not submit a tape represented three ego levels (3 at Self-aware, I-3/4; 13 at Conscientious, I-4; 3 at Individualistic, I-4/5) and each level of experience (4 at first practicum, 3 at second practicum, 12 at internship). Most of the policy restrictions involved students at the internship level, an unfortunate circumstance which may have limited the range of counseling behavior for analysis. Except for these restrictions, this study only includes student volunteers willing to be evaluated via an audiotape.

The lack of control over these extraneous variables may have also affected scores on the instruments. The

VPPS, for example, was devised for use with psychotherapy patients and may not have been an appropriate rating scale for some of the counselor-client interactions in this study, such as those related to career choice and school discipline. Client variance may also have affected supervisors' ratings of counselors; i.e., a student who was rated highly effective in one setting might have received a lower rating for the same performance in another setting. One supervisor noted that his student's rating was probably lowered because this practica (second) was her first experience with family therapy.

Limitations of the instruments themselves may also have affected the results of this study. First, the Sentence Completion Test used to measure ego level is a semiprojective instrument. Second, all of the instruments used in this study required some subjectivity in scoring. Judges rated responses to the sentence stems to measure ego level; judges classified perceptions of clients into the four content categories, judges rated interactions with clients based on three 5-minute segments from an audiotape of a single counseling session. Although all the raters had been trained by the suggested procedures and all the ratings had acceptable interrater reliability coefficients, the use of subjective ratings increases the chances of error. Third, measures of students' perceptions of their clients were based on self-report on a Rep Grid designed for this study, an otherwise untested variation of the technique.

The cross-sectional approach employed in this study prohibits any inferences to changes in counseling students' perceptions and behaviors as they gain experience or the impact of ego level on changes. The study did not address process dimensions of counseling students' development, but only examined sectors, naturally occurring groups of students at different levels of ego development with varying amounts of experience.

In addition, the generalizability of the results of this study are limited by its population, counseling students in one counselor education program. The University of Florida counseling program is relatively large, requires 72 semester hours for an Ed.S. degree, offers Ed.S. and Ph.D. degrees, and includes a diversity of special program areas. The results of this study may not be applicable to smaller programs with a particular focus, such as a masters' degree for school counseling.

This study was based in actual counseling sessions and actual supervisory relationships. Such a "real-life" investigation is desirable for exploratory research and has been suggested as the most appropriate approach to supervision education research at this beginning stage of investigation (Holloway & Hosford, 1983). But it is at the same time limited in its controls over extraneous variables, threats to internal and external validity.

Finally, ego development theory is broad and comprehensive in its scope. Its global nature perhaps restricts its ability to clearly differentiate between measures of specific cognitions and behaviors, especially for higher levels of ego development. Its greatest value may be its conceptual and richly descriptive nature, identifying specific attributes to be investigated, providing guidelines for designing curricula and supervision experiences, and describing a theoretical framework for an individual counseling student's development.

Discussion

This section includes a discussion of the results of the study, including whether or not they were anticipated and how the results of the various tests may relate to each other.

Structure of Students' Perceptions of Clients

Although the major hypotheses of this study concerning the relationship of counseling students' ego levels to the cognitive complexity, integration, and meaningfulness of their client construct systems were not supported, there is some evidence to suggest a different pattern of relationship than the one tested. Rather than having a linear relationship with ego level or a main effect in an analysis of differences between ego levels, cognitive complexity and integration seem to have an interactive nature, as proposed and investigated by Landfield (1977). Students at different ego levels tended to have client construct systems with

different combinations of high and low levels of complexity
and integration. They seemed to differ in their abilities
to differentiate between clients, to order their perceptions
in an hierarchial organization, and to use their perceptions
flexibly.

These differences did not relate to ego levels as
anticipated, however. The more complex and integrated
counseling students, those with more sophisticated and differentiated client construct systems, could be expected
theoretically to also be functioning at higher levels of
ego development. The finding that the least complex and
integrated counseling students, those with more rigid and
less flexible client construct systems, were also functioning at higher levels of ego development is a puzzle, however
These students would theoretically be expected to be at
lower ego levels characterized by more confined and simplistic thinking.

These differences in students' client construct systems are perhaps more meaningful when considered in conjunction with the content of the constructs. Counseling
students at high ego levels perceived their clients more
frequently in terms of the interactional style than did
students at lower ego levels. While the students at higher
ego levels differed in the structure of these perceptions--
i.e., some having highly differentiated and highly integrated client construct systems, some having much less
differentiated and integrated client construct systems--

these students had similar content in their perceptions--
i.e., interactional style. In contrast, students who had
either highly differentiated and poorly integrated or poorly
differentiated and highly integrated client construct systems were functioning at lower ego levels, and had similar
content--i.e., more psychological and physical descriptions
of their clients. Thus, it may not be sufficient to consider the structure alone of counseling students' perceptions of clients; the content of the perceptions may be a
critical variable for understanding the implications of the
degree of cognitive sophistication of those perceptions.
In other words, considering both structure and content may
prevent equating a client construct system of numerous, well
organized physical perceptions with a system of numerous
well organized interactional style perceptions.

Content of Students' Perceptions of Clients

While there was a significant difference in frequencies
of content categories of client constructs for counseling
students at different levels of ego development, the differences do not entirely follow Duck's (1973) continuum of
cognitive complexity, which would predict an increase in
frequency counts from physical to interactional to role to
psychological categories. The decrease in physical descriptions of clients is as expected, but the increase in interactional and decrease in psychological do not follow Duck's
continuum. These changes may be more appropriate, however,

for descriptions of clients as opposed to the changes in descriptions of friends across time periods in Duck's study. Counseling students at higher ego levels seem to have a higher awareness of the interactive nature of the counselor-client relationship and perhaps think of their clients more often in terms of this more sophisticated and subtle process than do students at lower ego levels.

Counseling students at the Self-aware (I-3/4) ego level primarily used psychological descriptions, perhaps reflective of their focus on feelings and internal states. In contrast, the Individualistic (I-4/5) students, who primarily used interactional descriptive statements, by definition understand mutuality in interpersonal relationships and are moving towards an increasing awareness of interdependency. The type of constructs generated by the students in each group thus seems a logical manifestation of their ego level.

Constructs within each of Duck's (1973) content category also reflected differences between ego levels. Psychological constructs especially varied in their degree of sophistication, from "unhappy-happy" and "low self-esteem-healthy sense of self-worth" and "bright-dull" (Self-aware), to "uncomfortable with sexuality (identity)-comfortable w/ sexuality and sexual identity," "feel responsible for self-feel responsible for others," and "self-determined, nondenial-denial projectionist" (Individualistic). Interactional descriptions ranged from descriptions of general style, "assertive-timid" (Self-aware) and "interpersonally engaging-interpersonally distant" (Individualistic), to those specific to the counselor-client relationship, such as "puts forth effort-refuses to try" (Self-aware), "wants counselor to 'fix' their problem-wants to work on fixing problem herself" (Conscientious),and "I was unable to express ideas I thought important; evoked similar defensive responses in me-One with whom I feel able to express anything I deem important" (Conscientious).

Physical descriptions included "upper middle class background-lower class background" (Conformist), "have children-no children" (Self-aware), "female-male" (Self-aware), "white-black" (Conscientious), and "terminally ill-physically healthy" (Individualistic).

None of the constructs described habitual activities or behaviors, part of Duck's (1973) role category. Some constructs classified in this category included stereotypic roles such as parent, wife, and student, while others referred to the client role. These client role descriptions were used by counseling students at all ego levels. They included diagnostic labels such as "PTSD patients-depressed and obsessive" (Conscientious), "psychotic-emotionally normal" (Individualistic), and "schizophrenic history-no schizophrenic history" (Individualistic); assessment statements such as "has multiple problems-does not have severe problems" (Self-aware) and "good prognosis for future-poor prognosis" (Conscientious);

specific issues such as "legal problems-family problems"
(Self-aware) and "homosexuality issues-heterosexuality
issues" (Conscientious); and process statements such as "'I
don't really want to change'-'Help me grow'" (Conscientious),
and "expected immediate results-understood that problems
were long in the making, treatment would be gradual and
lengthy" (Conscientious). All of one student's (Conscientious) constructs referred to the clients' cancer patient
roles.

In summary, while Duck's (1973) content categories
illustrated differences in client perceptions by ego
levels, the results of this study suggest a different continuum of cognitive complexity of client perceptions, one
in which interactional style is the most sophisticated.
Variation in perceptions within each category also appear
related to level of ego development.

Students' Counseling Behavior (VPPS)

Ratings of audiotapes of counseling students' behavior with their clients during a working counseling session
did not have a significant linear relationship with students'
levels of ego development in a regression analysis controlling for students' levels of experience. The analysis did,
however, suggest a near significant positive relationship,
with students at higher ego levels receiving higher VPPS
ratings. These results suggest that students functioning
at higher levels of ego development also tended to evidence

more therapist behavior and attitudes which have been related to positive therapy outcome, including warmth, emotional involvement, positive attitudes, and attempts to
examine clients' underlying psychodynamics. Ego development
theory implies increasing capacity for counseling-relevant
factors, such as responding empathically, dealing with
identity issues, understanding psychological causation and
paradox, recognizing themes and patterns of behavior, and
dealing with the interactive dynamics of the counselor-
client relationship. The near significant relationship of
VPPS ratings with EGO scores suggests students at higher
levels of ego development may be able to translate their
capacities into actual behavior with clients.

Supervisors' Effectiveness Ratings (CERS)

There was a trend for a positive relationship between
individual supervisors' ratings of students' counseling effectiveness and the students' ego levels. Students functioning at higher levels of ego development tended to be
rated as more effective overall by their supervisors, as
might be expected.

Counseling students' levels of experience, however, had
a significant curvilinear relationship with supervisors'
ratings, with students in second practica receiving the
lowest ratings. The lower scores of these students may
reflect different expectations of supervisors, or students
in second practica may have been attempting more advanced

skills for the first time. These are only speculations, however, and the results should be interpreted with caution because of the relatively smaller number of students in second practica, the large number of supervisors giving ratings, and the skewed (high) ratings in general.

Interestingly, VPPS and CERS ratings for 43 students were not significantly correlated ($r=.1231$, $p=.4317$). While the CERS is a broader instrument, based on students' performance in both counseling and supervision sessions, ratings of students' overall effectiveness might be expected to correlate with ratings of their in-session behaviors. This was not the case, however, in this study.

Conclusions, Implications, and Recommendations for Future Research

Most of the counseling students in this study were functioning at or above the Conscientious (I-4) level of ego development, the modal stage for graduate students identified by Swenson (1980b). Swenson (1980b) has suggested that to be effective counselors should be functioning at one level higher than their clients. If the modal level of young adults is Self-aware (I-3/4) (Loevinger & Knoll, 1983), these students seem capable of helping the majority of clients they may encounter in their practica and internship settings.

Most of the counseling students in this study had completed the major theoretical shift from Self-aware

(I-3/4) to Conscientious (I-4). This transition seems especially pertinent for counseling students. At the Self-aware stage, persons are beginning to differentiate self from others because of an increase in self-consciousness and self-awareness. They are moving beyond stereotypes to also begin to differentiate between other persons on a more individual basis. They describe interpersonal interactions in terms of feelings and traits.

These qualities are further developed by persons at the Conscientious (I-4) stage, so that their own internalized moral principles are the basis for self-evaluation. They now understand psychological causality and have a sense of a longer time perspective. They view interpersonal relations in terms of deeper feelings and the needs of others.

By definition, then, counseling students who have completed the transition from the Self-aware stage to the Conscientious stage have the capacity for making responsible ethical decisions, viewing clients as unique individuals, understanding the complex forces involved in counseling issues, and recognizing patterns and themes in clients' presentations of their problems.

Results of this study give initial support for the greater capacities for more effective counseling of persons at the Conscientious stage. Counseling students functioning at higher levels of ego development tended to be rated as more effective by their individual supervisors

(CERS). They also tended to have more differentiated, integrated, and flexible perceptions of their clients, and
they viewed their clients in terms of interactional dimensions. The trend in the results may be interpreted as
initial support for the theoretical hypotheses of the relationship between ego development and counselor development.
Further research is required, however, to challenge the null
hypotheses of no effect of a student's ego level on counseling performance. Further research should include modifications in design and statistical analysis which affected the
results of this study.

Of prime importance, efforts should be made in future
research to control the many extraneous variables in this
study. For example, a sample with more counseling students
at the extreme ego levels, especially pre-Conformist and
post-Conscientious stages, and more equal numbers of
students at each stage would allow for more reliable study
of the impact of ego level on counseling variables. Also
desirable is more control over the client population to
more specifically analyze the effect of counseling
students' ego levels on their responses to clients. Finally,
the use of fewer individual supervisors would help insure
more consistent ratings of counseling effectiveness.

The results of this study also suggest modifications
in the analysis of counseling variables based on the Rep
Grid. In particular, the "dual processes" (Landfield,
1977, p. 163) and interactive nature of cognitive complexity

and integration should be taken into consideration when choosing the statistical analysis for future studies. It also seems important to consider both the structure and content of counseling students' perceptions of their clients and to investigate any interactive processes between them. In addition, the wide variations within the content categories used to classify client constructs suggest a more complex classification system might distinguish more precisely between levels of sophistication of counseling students' perceptions of clients.

Results also indicate that, because of possible mediating effects, a counseling student's experience level should continue to be included in future studies. Developmental models of supervision education are based to some extent on anticipated changes as students gain experience (i.e., Littrell et al., 1979; Loganbill et al., 1982; Stoltenberg, 1981) and research based on these models (sometimes seeming to equate experience level and developmental level) have differentiated between students by experience levels (e.g., Heppner & Roehlke, 1984; Miars et al., 1983; Worthington, 1984). There were differences in the mean scores across levels of experience for several of the counseling variables in this study; the partial correlations computed in the statistical analyses controlled for these differences. Other effects of experience level were also noted. Supervisors' ratings (CERS), for example, had a significant curvilinear relationship with experience levels.

In the regression analysis which investigated the relationship of both ego levels (EGO) and experience levels (LEXP) with ratings of counseling behavior (VPPS), the two predictor variables together accounted for 14% of the variance of the ratings ($R^2=.1422$), while EGO controlling for LEXP accounted for 7% of the variance ($R^2=.0745$). The increase in mean VPPS ratings across experience levels seems logical, indicating more experienced students received higher ratings for counseling behavior related to positive outcome, and it parallels previous research which has suggested more experienced counselors have higher quality relationships with their clients (Hutchins, 1984).

Thus, while the effect of experience level should not be ignored, the impact of ego level on counseling performance also merits further investigation. The individual attributes of counseling students described by the theory of ego development appear to have an effect on their perceptions of and behavior with clients and may help explain individual variations in counselor development assumed by some developmental models of supervision education (Loganbill et al., 1982; Stoltenberg, 1981), and the individual differences within experience levels found in previous research (e.g., Friedlander & Snyder, 1983; Reising & Daniels, 1983).

Future studies using a longitudinal approach could address several questions related to this area of inquiry.

First, studies could investigate the effect of ego level
on changes in perceptions and behavior as counseling
students gain experience. For example, is there a developmental pattern of changes in the creation and modifi-
cation of the structure of counseling students' client
construct systems? Do students add a few new constructs
and then reorganize their client construct systems in
an on-going, successive-plateaus pattern? Loganbill et al.
(1982) have theorized such a circular process through
stages of stagnation, confusion, and integration as
students confront increasingly more complex counseling
issues. How might the student's ego level effect this
developmental sequence?

Other studies could try to identify whether there
is a similar pattern of changes in the content of counseling students' perceptions of clients and comparable influ-
ences of ego level on the pattern. A longitudinal study
of students' in-session counseling behavior could also
analyze how students' levels of ego development impact
their counseling performance as they gain experience
through their supervised practica and internships.

Another area for future research is how students
use their perceptions in making decisions about counseling interventions. Of interest would be whether this
process differs by ego level. Information processing
analysis is one possible approach to an investigation

of the link between cognitions and behavior of counseling
students.

Studies using longitudinal or information processing
approaches could have implications for counselor training
and supervision education. Curricula designs may need
to consider developmental patterns of changes in perceptions and behavior; training interventions may need to
focus on the translation of perceptions into behavior; both
curricula and interventions may need to include an assessment of individual traits of the counseling student as
identified by a student's level of ego development. Future
research is needed, however, to identify any relevant
training factors and the possible impact of ego level on
them.

Most of the counseling students in this study were
functioning at the Conscientious (I-4) stage of ego
development. If future studies verify this is the predominant ego level of graduate counseling students, as
suggested by Swenson (1980b), the characteristics of this
stage should be considered in designing curricula and
supervision experiences. Very different programs may be
needed for those counseling students at lower and higher
levels of ego development.

Summary

The results of this study suggest a highly complex
relationship between counseling students' level of ego

development and their perceptions of their clients, a relationship which intertwines ego level with the structure (cognitive complexity and integration) and content of students' perceptions. Counseling students' levels of ego development differentiated between their perceptions of their clients, tended to relate to the complexity, integration, and flexibility of these perceptions, tended to relate to supervisors' ratings of their overall counseling effectiveness, and tended to relate to ratings of students' in-session counseling behavior. The theory of ego development appears to have some merit as a basis for differentiating between counseling students' perceptions of and behavior with their clients and may provide some theoretical explanation for differences in students' progress through the developmental process of becoming a counselor.

The results also provide some theoretical support for the developmental models of supervision education which include the differential effects of counseling students' personal attributes in their developmental process. As suggested previously by other researchers (Bartlett, 1983; Holloway & Hosford, 1983; Kaplan, 1983; Lambert, 1980; Mahon & Altmann, 1977) and authors of developmental models of supervision education (Blocher, 1983; Loganbill et al., 1982; Stoltenberg, 1981), the issue at this point is not whether personal attributes affect counseling students' perceptions of and behavior with clients. Instead there is a need to address what the relevant attributes are and how they influence what happens during the counseling session. Answers to these questions will help counselor educators and supervisors design training and supervision interventions which can be effective in facilitating counseling students' development into competent counselors.

Role Titles

On your answer sheet, write the first name of a client who is best described by each statement. Write the names in the blanks provided at the top of each column. Name a client only once. Name a client for each description. Name clients you are currently seeing in your practicum or internship setting, or clients you have seen recently.[1]

1. The client who is/was most like you.

2. The client who is/was most unlike you.

3. The client for whom you feel/felt most sorry.

4. The client who is/was your greatest success.

5. The client who is/was the hardest for you to understand, or one you would consider a "failure."

6. The client from whom you are learning/learned the most.

7. The client with whom you feel/felt most comfortable.

8. The client who surprises/surprised you the most.

Constructs

Note that each row contains 3 circles. For each row, think of how two of the three clients indicated by the circles are alike or similar, and at the same time different from the third client. Write your description (a word or phrase) of how the two clients are <u>alike</u> or <u>similar</u> in the "Way Alike" column for that row. Then write the way in which the third client is <u>different</u> from the other two in the "Way Different" column. You might also think of the "Way Different" as the <u>opposite</u> of your description in the "Way Alike" column. Do this comparison and contrast for each row.

After you have completed the above, indicate for each pair of descriptions or constructs which is the most <u>positive</u> or your <u>preference</u> of the pair with a + sign in the parentheses beside that descriptor. Mark the other descriptor, the more <u>negative</u> one or the one you <u>prefer less</u>, with a - sign in the parentheses.

Finally, go back and rate each client on each pair of descriptions or constructs using the + and - values for a scale of -3 to +3·

-3 the negative construct strongly describes the client

-2 the negative construct describes the client

-1 the negative construct somewhat describes the client

+1 the positive construct somewhat describes the client

+2 the positive construct describes the client

+3 the positive construct strongly describes the client

Use a <u>zero</u> (0) rating if the constructs do not apply to the client, or if the two constructs are equally de-scriptive of the client.

Mark your ratings in the·boxes under the client's name which correspond to the constructs. Please mark <u>each</u> box.

---

[1]If first practicum students were not seeing a suffi-cient number of clients in their setting, they were asked to include persons they saw in prepracticum settings during the previous semester (i.e., in their Theories of Counseling and Principles of Counseling classes).

<u>Note</u>. Instructions were given orally and in the above written form in a semistructured interview format.

REPERTORY GRID TECHNIQUE--RESPONSE SHEET

CLIENTS' NAMES

CONSTRUCTS

WAY ALIKE

WAY DIFFERENT

(+) or (-)

APPENDIX B
LETTER TO STUDENTS

Dear

As a practicum or internship student this semester you
are eligible to participate in a study of counselor development. My dissertation is designed to explore and describe
how counselors at different stages of their educational experience view their clients and interact with their clients.

Your participation in this study will involve the
following:

1. Complete two assessment instruments.
    (Dissertations require concrete data; so does the
    computer.) One will ask you how you think about
    your clients. The second is a more open-ended
    instrument.

2. Submit an (audible!) audiotape of the third
    session with the client of your choice. The
    tapes will be analyzed to describe how counselors
    interact with their clients. Enclosed is a re-
    lease form for the client you choose to sign.
    You will be given a tape to use.

3. Agree to allow your individual supervisor to
    complete an evaluation scale at the end of the
    semester.

If you choose to participate, you will be asked to
complete the two instruments in small group meetings at a
time convenient to you. Testing should take a maximum of
1 to 1-1/2 hours, allowing you plenty of time to think
about responses. You can bring the audiotape and client
release form to that meeting.

At the beginning of our small group meeting, you will
be assigned an identification number. Only that number
will appear on your testing instruments and tape. Evaluation forms mailed to your individual supervisors will also
only be marked with your identification number. None of
the raters who score the instruments or tapes will have any
obvious means to identify the "author." Raters will be

145

doctoral students in counselor education and clinical
psychology, and a recent Ph.D. graduate of the counselor
education program (all friendly and highly ethical). At
no time will your host, individual supervisors, or group
supervisor have access to any of your data. Your answers
on the instruments and your tape will in no way be related
to your grade for your practicum/internship.

I will be contacting you by phone in the next week to
schedule the group meeting for those who agree to participate in this study. I will want to answer any questions
you have about the study, so please ask them when I call.

I won't be able to list all of your names in my dissertation Acknowledgements section (I need an N of 60!),
but your participation will be acknowledged as a group in
writing and appreciated personally--sincerely.

I look forward to talking with you and meeting with
you soon. At any time during the study you may contact me
at 392-0721 (134 Norman Hall) and/or 373-9637 (home).

Thank you for your help

Sincerely,

L. DiAnne Borders
Doctoral Candidate
Department of Counselor
Education

Enclosure

APPENDIX C
CLIENT RELEASE FORM

University of Florida
Department of Counselor Education

Subject's Name_____

Subject's Address_____

Project Title An Application of Ego Development Theory to
               Counselor Development and Supervision Educa-
               tion

Principal Investigator Leslie DiAnne Borders Date_____

I agree to participate in the research as explained below:

     The purpose of this study is to explore and describe
how counselors at different stages of their education experience view their clients and interact with their clients. To
participate you will need to do the following:

     Allow your counselor to audiotape your third counsel-
     ing session. This tape will be analyzed to describe
     how counselors interact with their clients. Your
     participation will be completely anonymous to the
     researcher and reviewers of the tape.

     Please feel free to ask any question which you may
     have at this time.

The above stated nature and purpose of this research, including discomforts, and risks involved (if any) have been
explained to me. Furthermore, I understand that this investigation may be used for educational purposes which may
include publication. I also understand that I may withdraw
my consent at any time without prejudice.

This information will be kept confidential within legal
limits (or to the extent provided by law).

                         Signed_____

I have defined and explained fully this research to the
participant whose signature appears above.

                         Signed_____

APPENDIX D
STUDENT RELEASE FORM

University of Florida
Department of Counselor Education

Subject's Name_____

Subject's Address_____

Project Title__An Application of Ego Development Theory to__
              __Counselor Development and Supervision Educa-__
              __tion__

Principal Investigator__Leslie DiAnne Borders__ Date_____

I agree to participate in the research as explained below:

The purpose of this study is to explore and describe
how counselors at different stages of their education experience view their clients and interact with their clients.
To participate you will need to do the following:

1. Complete 2 assessment instruments. One will ask
   you how you think about your clients. The second
   is a more open-ended and general instrument. This
   will take approximately 1 to 1-1/2 hours to complete.

2. Submit an audiotape of the third session with the
   client of your choice. The tapes will be analyzed
   to describe how counselors interact with their
   clients. You will be provided with an audiotape
   to use.

3. Agree to allow your individual supervisor to
   complete an evaluation scale at the end of the
   semester.

Please feel free to ask any question which you may
have at this time.

The above stated nature and purpose of this research, including discomforts, and risks involved (if any) have been
explained to me. Furthermore, I understand that this
investigation may be used for educational purposes which
may include publication. I also understand that I may
withdraw my consent at any time without prejudice.

This information will be kept confidential within legal
limits (or to the extent provided by law).

Signed_____

I have defined and explained fully this research to the
participant whose signature appears above.

Signed_____

APPENDIX E
DATA SHEET

Name_____ Identification Number _____

Address_____ Phone Number_____

Age____ Race____ Sex____ Date_____

Please indicate the following:

I am enrolled in __1st Practicum __2nd Practicum __Internship

Setting_____

Individual Supervisor_____

Counselor Education program/track_____

___Ed.S. ___Ed.D. ___Ph.D.

Previous experience in the helping professions (please indicate all your experiences)

___years--Counselor (Setting_____)

___years--Teaching (Grade level_____)

___years--Student personnel/Student Services (Setting____)

___years--Social work (Setting_____)

___years--Medical (Please specify_____Setting_____)

___years--Volunteer work (Please specify_____)

___years--Other (Please specify_____)

Professional plans_____

APPENDIX F
LETTER TO INDIVIDUAL SUPERVISORS

Dear

        Your individual supervisee,   , has
agreed to participate in my dissertation study One part
of that agreement is allowing me to ask you to complete an
evaluation scale of the student's work at the end of this
semester.

        The study is designed to explore how counselors at
different stages of their educational experience perceive
and interact with their clients, and how effective they are
with their clients. I am asking you to complete the
Counselor Evaluation Rating Scale (CERS) (Myrick & Kelly,
1971) as a dependent measure of counselor effectiveness.
The CERS is made up of 27 Likert-type (-3 to +3) items
designed to assess the counselor's behavior in both counseling and supervision sessions. The CERS takes approximately 15 minutes to complete.

        If you agree to complete the CERS for your individual
supervisee(s), I will mail a copy for each supervisee to
you during the tenth week of the semester along with a
stamped, self-addressed envelope.

        If you have any questions concerning the study and/or
your participation, please call me at 373-9637 or 392-0721.

        Thank you for your help with this research project.

                        Sincerely,

                        DiAnne Borders
                        Doctoral Candidate
                        Department of Counselor
                          Education

Dear

   Thank you for agreeing to participate in my dissertation study, an exploratory investigation of counselors'
perceptions of and interactions with clients.

   Enclosed is the Counselor Evaluation Rating Scale
(CERS), the dependent measure of counselor effectiveness in
my study. Please complete an evaluation for each of your
supervisee(s), listed below, who volunteered to participate in the study and agreed to allow me to ask you to
complete the CERS. The CERS is marked with the supervisee's identification number only. Please return the
completed CER(s) to me in the self-addressed, stamped envelope within one week.

   My study should be completed by late June and I would
be glad to share the results with you at that time. Please
indicate below if you would like a copy of the results
mailed to you.

   If you have any questions, please call me at 373-9637
or 392-0721.

   I appreciate your time and help.

                        Sincerely,

                        L. DiAnne Borders
                        Doctoral Candidate
                        Department of Counselor
                        Education

Please mail me a copy of the results of the study.
Name_____
Address_____
Individual Supervisee(s):

APPENDIX H
TWO-WAY ANALYSIS OF VARIANCE OF LEVELS OF EGO
DEVELOPMENT WITH COGNITIVE COMPLEXITY (FIC)
AND COGNITIVE INTEGRATION (ORD)

Sources	SS	df	MS	F	p
FIC	5.5313	1	5.5313	0.03	.8717
ORD	68.7195	1	68.7195	0.33	.5698
FIC X ORD	547.1631	1	547.1631	2.60	.1121
Error	12408.6767	59	210.3166		

Note. FIC = Functionally Independent Construction (cognitive complexity); ORD = Ordination score (cognitive integration).

APPENDIX I
SIMPLE REGRESSION ANALYSIS OF SUPERVISORS'
EFFECTIVENESS RATINGS (CERS) WITH LEVELS
OF EGO DEVELOPMENT (EGO)

Sources	SS	df	MS	F	p	R^2
EGO	1533.3191	1	1533.3191	2.97	.0907	.051153
Error	28441.5581	55	517.1192			

Note. EGO = Level of ego development (item sum scores).

154

APPENDIX J
POLYNOMIAL REGRESSION ANALYSIS OF SUPERVISORS'
EFFECTIVENESS RATINGS (CERS) WITH LEVELS OF
EXPERIENCE (LEXP)

Sources	SS	df	MS	F	p	R^2
LEXP	1773.3024	1	1773.3024	3.53	.0657	.094469
SQLEXP	2038.4576	1	2038.4576	4.06	.0490	
Error	27143.2746	54	502.6514			

Note. LEXP = Level of experience; SQLEXP = Level of experience, quadratic term. The R^2 coefficient is for the regression equation including LEXP and SQLEXP.

REFERENCES

Adams-Webber, J. R., Schwenker, B., & Barbeau, D. (1972).
    Personal constructs and the perception of individual
    differences. Canadian Journal of Behavioural Science,
    4, 218-224.

Atkins, S. R. (1976). Experiencing and ego development
    (Doctoral dissertation, University of Chicago, 1976).
    Dissertation Abstracts International, 37, 3058B.

Banikiotes, P. G. (1977). The training of counseling psy-
    chologists. The Counseling Psychologist, 7 (2), 23-26.

Bartlett, W. E. (1983). A multidimensional framework for
    the analysis of supervision of counseling. The
    Counseling Psychologist, 11 (1), 9-17.

Bartlett, W. E., Goodyear, R. K., & Bradley, F. O. (Eds.).
    (1983). Supervision in counseling II [Special issue].
    The Counseling Psychologist, 11 (1).

Ben-Peretz, M., & Katz, S. (1983, July). From simplicity
    to complexity: Differences in the construct systems
    of student-teachers. Paper presented at the meeting
    of the Fifth International Congress on Personal
    Construct Psychology, Boston, MA.

Bernard, J. M. (1979). Supervisory training: A discrimina-
    tion model Counselor Education and Supervision, 19,
    60-68.

Bernier, J. E. (1980). Training and supervising counselors:
    Lessons learned from deliberate psychological educa-
    tion. Personnel and Guidance Journal, 59, 15-20.

Blaas, C. D., & Heck, E. J. (1978). Selected process vari-
    ables as a function of client type and cognitive com-
    plexity in beginning counselors. Journal of Counseling
    Psychology, 25, 257-263.

Blocher, D. H. (1983). Toward a cognitive developmental
    approach to counseling supervision. The Counseling
    Psychologist, 11 (1), 27-34.

Blocher, D. H., & Wolleat, P. (1974). Some reactions to
    Zifferblatt and a report of a practical attempt at the

development and evaluation of a counselor education mode. The Counseling Psychologist, 3, 35-55.

Bochini, M. T. (1978). The organization of value systems at different stages of ego development (Doctoral dissertation, Catholic University of America, 1977). Dissertation Abstracts International, 38, 3362B. (University Microfilms No. 77-27,712)

Borman, C. A., & Ramirez, C. (1975). Evaluating counseling practicum students. Counselor Education and Supervision, 15, 48-54.

Boyd, J. B. (1978). Counselor supervision: Approaches, preparation, practice. Muncie, IN: Accelerated Development.

Brown, R. G. (1970). A study of the perceptual organization of elementary and secondary outstanding young educators (Doctoral dissertation, University of Florida, 1970). Dissertation Abstracts International, 32, 1328A.

Carlozzi, A. F., Gaa, J. P., & Liberman, D. B. (1983). Empathy and ego development. Journal of Counseling Psychology, 30, 113-116.

Carr, J. E. (1980). Personal construct theory and psychotherapy research. In A. W. Landfield & L. M. Leitner (Eds.), Personal construct psychology: Psychotherapy and personality, New York: Wiley.

Casas, J. M., Brady, S., & Ponterotto, J. G. (1983). Sexual preference bias in counseling: An information processing approach. Journal of Counseling Psychology, 30, 139-145.

Cichetti, D., & Ornston, P. S. (1976). The initial psychotherapy interview: A content analysis of the verbal responses of novice and experienced therapists. Journal of Psychology, 93, 167-174.

Cognetta, P. (1977). Deliberate psychological education: A high school cross-age teaching model. Counseling Psychologist, 6, 22-25.

Combs, A. W. (1969). Florida studies in the helping profession. University of Florida Social Science Monograph, 37. Gainesville, FL; University of Florida Press.

Combs, A. W., Richards, A. C., & Richards, F. (1976). Perceptual psychology: A humanistic approach to the study of persons. New York: Harper & Row.

Cooper, T. D., & Lewis, J. A. (1983). The crisis of relativism: Helping counselors cope with diversity. Counselor Education and Supervision, 22, 290-295.

Copeland, W. D. (1982). Student teachers' preference for supervisory approach. Journal of Teacher Education, 33, 32-36.

Copeland, W. D., & Atkinson, D. R. (1978). Student teachers' perceptions of directive and non-directive supervisory behavior. Journal of Educational Research, 71, 123-127.

Cox, N. (1974). Prior health, ego development and helping behavior. Child Development, 45, 594-603.

Cross, D. G., & Brown, D. (1983). Counselor supervision as a function of trainee experience: Analysis of specific behaviors. Counselor Education and Supervision, 22, 333-341.

Dedrick, C. (1972). The relationship between perceptual characteristics and effective teaching at the junior college level (Doctoral Dissertation, University of Florida, 1972). Dissertation Abstracts International, 33, 4170A-4171A.

Duck, S. W. (1973). Personal relationships and personal constructs· A study of friendship formation. New York: Wiley.

Duehn, W. D., & Proctor, E. K. (1974). A study of cognitive complexity in the education for social work practice. Journal of Education for Social Work, 10, 20-26.

Erickson, V. L. (1975). Deliberate psychological education for women: From Iphigenia to Antigone. Counselor Education and Supervision, 14, 297-309.

Erickson, V. L. (1977). Beyond Cinderella: Ego maturity and attitudes toward the rights and roles of women. Counseling Psychologist, 7, 83-88. (a)

Erickson, V. L. (1977). Deliberate psychological education for women: A curriculum follow-up study. Counseling Psychologist, 6 (4), 25-29. (b)

Exum, H. A. (1979). Cross-age and peer teaching: A deliberate psychological education curriculum for junior college students (Doctoral dissertation, University of Minnesota, 1978). Dissertation Abstracts International, 39, 672A-673A. (University Microfilms No. 7813393)

Fransella, F., & Bannister, D. (1977). A manual for Repertory Grid Technique. New York: Academic Press.

Friedlander, M. L., & Snyder, J. (1983). Trainee's expectations for the supervisory process: Testing a developmental model. Counselor Education and Supervision, 22, 342-348.

Gilligan, C. (1982). In a different voice: Psychological theory and women's development. Cambridge: Harvard University Press.

Glassberg, S. (1978). Peer supervision for student teachers: A cognitive-developmental approach to teacher education (Doctoral dissertation, University of Minnesota, 1977). Dissertation Abstracts International, 38, 6068A. (University Microfilms No. 7802669)

Goldberg, A. (1974). Conceptual system as a predisposition toward therapeutic communication. Journal of Counseling Psychology, 21, 364-368.

Gomes-Schwartz, B. (1978). Effective ingredients in psychotherapy: Prediction of outcome from process variables. Journal of Consulting and Clinical Psychology, 46, 1023-1035.

Gore, M. R. (1978). The relationship of dogmatism and conceptual system to supervisor ratings of counseling effectiveness (Doctoral dissertation, University of Toledo, 1977). Dissertation Abstracts International, 38, 6533A-6534A. (University Microfilms No. 7802484).

Grayson, D. S. (1979). Approach to supervision, tolerance of ambiguity and level of training (Doctoral dissertation, University of Utah, 1979). Dissertation Abstracts International, 40, 108A. (University Microfilms No. 7915848)

Gurk, M. D., & Wicas, E. A. (1979). Generic models of counseling supervision: Counseling/instruction dichotomy and consultation metamodel. Personnel and Guidance Journal, 57, 402-407.

Hansen, J. C., Pound, R., & Petro, C. (1976). Review of research on practicum supervision. Counselor Education and Supervision, 16, 107-116.

Hansen, J. C., Robins, T. H., & Grimes, J. (1982). Review of research on practicum supervision. Counselor Education and Supervision, 22, 15-24.

Hansen, J. C., & Warner, R. W., Jr. (1971). Review of research on practicum supervision. Counselor Education and Supervision, 10, 261-272.

Hart, G. M. (1982). The process of clinical supervision Baltimore, MD: University Park Press.

Harvey, O. J., Hunt, D. E., & Schroder, H. M. (1961). Conceptual systems and personality organization. New York. Wiley.

Hauser, S. T. (1976). Loevinger's model and measure of ego development: A critical review. Psychological Bulletin, 83, 928-955.

Heck, E. J., & Davis, C. S. (1973). Differential expression of empathy in a counseling analogue. Journal of Counseling Psychology, 20, 101-104.

Heppner, P. P., & Roehlke, H. J. (1984). Differences among supervisees at different levels of training· Implications for a developmental model of supervision. Journal of Counseling Psychology, 31, 76-90.

Hess, A. K. (Ed.). (1980). Psychotherapy supervision: Theory, research and practice. New York: Wiley. (a)

Hess, A. K. (1980). Training models and the nature of psychotherapy supervision. In A. K. Hess (Ed.), Psychotherapy supervision: Theory, research and practice. New York: Wiley. (b)

Hill, C. E., Charles, D., & Reed, K. G. (1981). A longitudinal analysis of changes in counseling skills during doctoral training in counseling psychology. Journal of Counseling Psychology, 28, 428-436.

Hirsch, P. A., & Stone, G. L. (1982). Attitudes and behavior in counseling skill development. Journal of Counseling Psychology, 29, 516-522.

Hogan, R. A. (1964). Issues and approaches in supervision. Psychotherapy: Theory, research and practice, 1, 139-141.

Holloway, E. L. (1979). The effects of conceptual level on clinical hypothesis formation and the supervision interview (Doctoral dissertation, University of Wisconsin, 1979). Dissertation Abstracts International, 40, 3121A. (University Microfilms No. 31-31,30)

Holloway, E. L., & Hosford, R. E. (1983). Towards developing a prescriptive technology of counselor supervision. The Counseling Psychologist, 11 (1), 73-77.

Hoppe, C. F., & Loevinger, J. (1977). Ego development and conformity: A construct validity study of the Washington University Sentence Completion Test. *Journal of Personality Assessment, 41*, 497-504.

Hunt, D. E. (1971). *Matching models in education: The coordination of teaching methods with student characteristics.* Toronto: Ontario Institute for Studies in Education.

Hunt, D. E., & Sullivan, E. V. (1974). *Between psychology and education.* Hinsdale, IL: Dryden Press.

Hurt, B. L. (1977). Psychological education for teacher education students: A cognitive-developmental curriculum. *Counseling Psychologist, 6*, 57-60.

Hutchins, D. E. (1984). Improving the counseling relationship. *Personnel and Guidance Journal, 62*, 572-575.

Jones, L. K. (1974). The Counselor Evaluation Rating Scale: A valid criterion of counselor effectiveness? *Counselor Education and Supervision, 14*, 112-116.

Kaplan, D. M. (1983). Current trends in practicum supervision research. *Counselor Education and Supervision, 22*, 215-226.

Kelly, G. A. (1955). *The psychology of personal constructs* (Vols. 1-2). New York: Norton.

Kimberlin, C., & Friesen, D. (1977). Effects of client ambivalence, trainee conceptual level, and empathy training conditions on empathic responding. *Journal of Counseling Psychology, 24*, 354-358.

Kimberlin, C. L., & Friesen, D. D. (1980). Sex and conceptual level empathic responses to ambivalent affect. *Counselor Education and Supervision, 19*, 252-258.

Kohlberg, L. (1969). Stage and sequence: The cognitive-developmental approach to socialization. In D. Goslin (Ed.), *Handbook of socialization theory and research.* Chicago: Rand-McNally.

Kohlberg, L., & Wasserman, E. R. (1980). The cognitive-developmental approach and the practicing counselor: An opportunity for counselors to rethink their roles. *Personnel and Guidance Journal, 58*, 559-567.

Lambert, M. J. (1980). Research and the supervisory process. In A. K. Hess (Ed.), *Psychotherapy supervision: Theory, research and practice.* New York: Wiley.

Landfield, A. W. (1971). Personal construct systems in psychotherapy. Chicago: Rand McNally.

Landfield, A. W. (1977). Interpretive man: The enlarged self-image. In A. W. Landfield, (Ed.), Nebraska Symposium on Motivation 1976. Lincoln, NE: University of Nebraska Press.

Lasker, H. (1978). Ego development and motivation: A cross-cultural cognitive-developmental analysis of n achievement (Doctoral dissertation, University of Chicago, 1978). Dissertation Abstracts International, 39, 2013B. (University Microfilms No. not given).

Leddick, G. R., & Bernard, J. M. (1980). The history of supervision: A critical review. Counselor Education and Supervision, 19, 186-196.

Lichtenberg, J. W., & Heck, E. J. (1979). Interactional structure of interviews conducted by counselors of differing levels of cognitive complexity. Journal of Counseling Psychology, 26, 15-22.

Lifshitz, M. (1974). Quality professionals: Does training make a difference? A personal construct theory study of the issue. British Journal of Social and Clinical Psychology, 13, 183-189.

Littrell, J. M. (1978). Concerns of beginning counselor trainees. Counselor Education and Supervision, 18, 29-35.

Littrell, J. M., Lee-Borden, N., & Lorenz, J. (1979). A developmental framework for counseling supervision. Counselor Education and Supervision, 19, 129-136.

Loesch, L. C., & Rucker, B. B. (1977). A factor analysis of the Counselor Evaluation Rating Scale. Counselor Education and Supervision, 16, 209-216.

Loevinger, J. (1966). The meaning and measurement of ego development. American Psychologist, 21, 195-206.

Loevinger, J. (1976). Ego development. San Francisco: Jossey-Bass.

Loevinger, J. (1979). Construct validity of the Sentence Completion Test of Ego Development. Applied Psychological Measurement, 3, 281-311.

Loevinger, J. (1980). Some thoughts on ego development and counseling. Personnel and Guidance Journal, 58, 389-390.

Loevinger, J., & Knoll, E. (1983). Personality: Stages, traits, and the self. Annual Review of Psychology, 34, 195-222.

Loevinger, J., & Wessler, R. (1970). Measuring ego development (Vol. 1). San Francisco: Jossey-Bass.

Loevinger, J., Wessler, R., & Redmore, C. (1970). Measuring ego development (Vol. 2). San Francisco: Jossey-Bass.

Loganbill, C., Hardy, E., & Delworth, U. (1982). Supervision: A conceptual model. The Counseling Psychologist, 10 (1), 3-42.

Lutwak, N., & Hennessy, J. J. (1982). Conceptual systems functioning as a mediating factor in the development of counseling skills. Journal of Counseling Psychology, 29, 256-260.

Mahon, B. R., & Altmann, H. S. (1977). Skill training: Cautions and recommendations. Counselor Education and Supervision, 17, 42-50.

Miars, R. D., Tracey, T. J., Ray, P. B., Cornfeld, J. L., O'Farrell, M., & Gelso, C. J. (1983). Variation in supervision process across trainee experience levels. Journal of Counseling Psychology, 30, 403-412.

Miller, R. (1982). Commentary--Supervision: A conceptual model. The Counseling Psychologist, 10 (1), 47-48.

Mosher, R. L., & Sprinthall, N. A. (1971). Psychological education: A means to promote personal development during adolescence. Counseling Psychologist, 2 (4), 3-82.

Moskowitz, S. A. (1981). A developmental model for the supervision of psychotherapy: The effect of level of experience on trainees' views of ideal supervision (Doctoral dissertation, Loyola University, 1981). Dissertation Abstracts International, 42, 1184B-1185B. (University Microfilms No. 8119985)

Murphy, P. D., & Brown, M. M. (1970). Conceptual system and teaching style. American Educational Research Journal, 7, 529-540.

Myrick, R. D., & Kelly, F. D., Jr. (1971). A scale for evaluating practicum students in counseling and supervision. Counselor Education and Supervision, 10, 330-336.

Nash, V. C. (1975). The clinical supervision of psychotherapy (Doctoral dissertation, Yale University, 1975).
Dissertation Abstracts International, 36, 2480B-
2481B. (University Microfilms No. 75-24,581)

Neimeyer, G. J., & Neimeyer, R. A. (1981). Personal con-
struct perspectives on cognitive assessment. In
T. Merluzzi, C. Glass, and M. Genest (Eds.), Cognitive
Assessment. New York: Guilford.

Nelson, G. L. (1978). Psychotherapy supervision from the
trainee's point of view: A survey of preferences.
Professional Psychology, 9, 539-550.

Oja, S. N., & Sprinthall, N. A. (1978). Psychological and
moral development for teachers: Can you teach old
dogs? Character Potential: A Record of Research, 8,
218-225.

O'Malley, S. S., Suh, C. S., & Strupp, H. H. (1983). The
Vanderbilt Psychotherapy Process Scale: A report on
the scale development and a process-outcome study.
Journal of Consulting and Clinical Psychology, 51,
581-586.

Perry, W. G., Jr. (1970). Forms of intellectual and ethical development in the college years. New York:
Holt, Rinehart, & Winston.

Philip, A. E., & McCulloch, J. W. (1968). Personal construct theory and social work practice. British
Journal of Social and Clinical Psychology, 7, 115-121.

Pope, M. L., & Keen, T. R. (1981). Personal construct
psychology and education. New York: Academic Press.

Reising, G. N., & Daniels, M. H. (1983). A study of
Hogan's model of counselor development and supervision.
Journal of Counseling Psychology, 30, 235-244.

Rest, J. R. (1980). Moral judgment research and the
cognitive-developmental approach to moral education.
Personnel and Guidance Journal, 58, 602-605.

Reynolds, R. S. (1981). Effective psychotherapy supervision as perceived by psychology interns (Doctoral
dissertation, The American University, Washington,
DC, (1980). Dissertation Abstracts International, 41,
4684B-4685B. (University Microfilms No. 8110116)

Rock, M. (1975). Self-reflection and ego development
(Doctoral dissertation, New York University, 1975).
Dissertation Abstracts International, 36, 3066B.
(University Microfilms No. 75-28,583)

Rogers, C. R. (1961). On becoming a person. Boston: Houghton Mifflin.

Rosenthal, N. R. (1977). A prescriptive approach for counselor training. Journal of Counseling Psychology, 24, 231-237.

Rotter, J. C. (1972). The perceptual characteristics of elementary, secondary and community college counselors (Doctoral dissertation, Wayne State University, 1971). Dissertation Abstracts International, 32, 6137A. (University Microfilms No. 72-14,613)

Runkel, P. J., & Damrin, D. E. (1961). Effects of training and anxiety upon teachers' preference information about students. Journal of Educational Psychology, 52, 254-261.

Rustad, K., & Rogers, C. (1975). Promoting psychological growth in a high school class. Counselor Education and Supervision, 14, 277-285.

Ryle, A., & Breen, D. (1974). Change in the course of social work training: A repertory grid study. British Journal of Medical Psychology, 47, 139-147.

Schenberg, R. G. (1974). The relation of time perspective and self-actualization to ego development (Doctoral dissertation, Washington University, 1973). Dissertation Abstracts International, 34, 4641B. (University Microfilms No. 74-07,064)

Schmidt, J. A., & Davison, M. L. (1983). Helping students think. Personnel and Guidance Journal, 61, 563-569.

Sebes, J. M., & Ford, D. H. (1984). Moral development and self-regulation: Research and intervention planning. Personnel and Guidance Journal, 62, 379-382.

Spooner, S. S., & Stone, S. C. (1977). Maintenance of specific counseling skills over time. Journal of Counseling Psychology, 24, 66-71.

Stoltenberg, C. (1981). Approaching supervision from a developmental perspective: The counselor complexity model. Journal of Counseling Psychology, 28, 59-65.

Strohmer, D. C., Biggs, D. A., Haase, R. F., & Purcell, M. J. (1983). Training counselors to work with disabled clients: Cognitive and affective components. Counselor Education and Supervision, 23, 132-141.

166

Strupp, H. H. (1981). Vanderbilt Psychotherapy Process
Scales (VPPS): Rater manual (rev. ed.). Unpublished
manuscript, Vanderbilt University, Nashville.

Suh, C. S , O'Malley, S. S., & Strupp, H. H (in press).
The Vanderbilt process measures: The Psychotherapy
Process Scale (VPPS) and the Negative Indicators Scale
(VNIS). In L. S. Greenberg & W. M. Pinsof (Eds.),
The psychotherapeutic process: A research handbook.
New York: Guilford Press

Sullivan, P. J. (1975). A curriculum for stimulating moral
reasoning and ego development in adolescents (Doctoral
dissertation, Boston University, 1975). Dissertation
Abstracts International, 1975, 36, 1320A. (University
Microfilms No. 75-20,971)

Swenson, C. H. (1977). Ego development and the interpersonal relationship. In D. Nevill (Ed.), Humanistic
psychology; New frontiers. New York: Gardner.

Swenson, C. H. (1980). Ego development. In R. H. Woody
(Ed.), Encyclopedia of clinical assessment. San
Francisco: Jossey-Bass. (a)

Swenson, C. H. (1980). Ego development and a general model
for counseling and psychotherapy. Personnel and
Guidance Journal, 58, 382-388. (b)

Van Hoose, W. H., & Paradise, L. V. (1979). Ethics in
counseling and psychotherapy. Cranston, RI: Carroll
Press.

Vonk, H. G. (1970). The relationship of teacher effectiveness to perception of self and teaching purpose
(Doctoral dissertation, University of Florida, 1970).

Wampold, B. E., Casas, J. M., & Atkinson, D. R. (1981).
Ethic bias in counseling. Journal of Counseling
Psychology, 28, 498-503.

Welfel, E. R., & Lipsitz, N. E. (1983). Ethical orientation of counselors: Its relationship to moral reasoning and level of training. Counselor Education and
Supervision, 23, 35-45. (a)

Welfel, E. R., & Lipsitz, N. E. (1983) Wanted: A comprehensive approach to ethics research and education.
Counselor Education and Supervision, 22, 320-332. (b)

Widick, C. (1977). The Perry scheme: A foundation for
developmental practice. Counseling Psychologist, 6,
35-38.

Worthington, E. L., Jr. (1984). Empirical investigation of supervision of counselors as they gain experience. Journal of Counseling Psychology, 31, 63-75.

Worthington, E. L., Jr., & Roehlke, H. J. (1979). Effective supervision as perceived by beginning counselors-in-training. Journal of Counseling Psychology, 26, 64-73.

Zahner, C. J., & McDavis, R. J. (1980). Moral development of professional and paraprofessional counselors and trainees. Counselor Education and Supervision, 19, 243-251.

Zielinski, C. E. (1973). Stage of ego development as a correlate of ability in discrimination and communication of empathic understanding (Doctoral dissertation, University of Houston, 1973). Dissertation Abstracts International, 34, 1635A. (University Microfilms No. 73-22,941)

BIOGRAPHICAL SKETCH

Leslie DiAnne Borders was born April 7, 1950, and lived in various areas of North Carolina for the next 31 years. She graduated from the University of North Carolina at Greensboro in 1972 with a B.A. in English, then taught high school English courses at High Point Central High School for five years. She received a M.A.Ed. in counseling from Wake Forest University in Winston-Salem, North Carolina, in 1979, where she completed a year-long internship at the Center for Psychological Services and served as a graduate assistant and an adjunct instructor for the Department of Education. Sne was a counselor at the Lifespan Center, Salem College and Academy, in historic Old Salem, for two years before moving to Gainesville, Florida, to enter graduate school in 1981. During her doctoral program at the University of Florida she completed internship experiences in counseling, teaching, research, and supervision, and served one year as the chair of the national ACES Graduate Student Committee. Beginning Fall 1984 she will be Assistant Professor of Counselor Education at Oakland University, Rochester, Michigan.

I certify that I have read this study and that in my opinion it conforms to acceptable standards of scholarly presentation and is fully adequate, in scope and quality, as a dissertation for the degree of Doctor of Philosophy.

Dr. Margaret L. Fong, Chairperson
Assistant Professor of Counselor
Education

I certify that I have read this study and that in my opinion it conforms to acceptable standards of scholarly presentation and is fully adequate, in scope and quality, as a dissertation for the degree of Doctor of Philosophy.

Dr. P. Joseph Wittmer,
Cochairperson
Professor of Counselor Education

I certify that I have read this study and that in my opinion it conforms to acceptable standards of scholarly presentation and is fully adequate, in scope and quality, as a dissertation for the degree of Doctor of Philosophy.

Dr. Gregory J. Neimeyer
Assistant Professor of Psychology

CPSIA information can be obtained
at www.ICGtesting.com
Printed in the USA
LVOW03s1500210716

497243LV00017B/271/P